Pr

... a fast-paced cou...... .e palpable tension between a defendant and victims, but also lays bare the internal conflict between the judge, counsel, law enforcement, and experts. The historically accurate discussion of domestic violence exposes residual issues that still draw a shadow over justice today. While the author often refers to his "luck," preparation is the mother of luck. Every trial lawyer should enjoy reading how the author created his own luck through diligence and hard work.

   – Philip E. Rodgers Jr., 13th Circuit Court judge (retired)

My gratitude to Mr. Steadman for writing this important and dramatically told novel. People need to know the long-term, horrible effects that physical and sexual abuse does to a person. My hope is that victims speak out about their experiences and end society's insistence of sweeping these assaults under the rug.

   – Joni Ankerson, author of *To Kill or Be Killed: A True Crime*
     Memoir from Prison

... Through his main character's reflections on events in Darien, Steadman captures perfectly many of the aspects of small-town living, where everybody went to the same high school and knows one another's business. And through the slow, step-by-step dramatization of the trial, the author wonderfully elicits the workaday, real-world lessons of a career in the law. Steadman deftly escalates the drama both inside and outside the courtroom, and the display of his legal skills in the former setting neatly counterbalances the simple sweetness of how he handles the latter. An effective and engaging legal tale about the trial of an abused wife.

   –*Kirkus Reviews*

I Killed Sam is a chilling story of wife abuse and murder based on a case that Mr. Steadman defended in 1957. He is a brilliant attorney whom I have personally observed win a series of jury trials over 40 years, including a $400,000 jury award against a local bank at the age of eighty. I recommend it as required reading in law schools and history classes.

   – Larry E. Lelito, author of *True Hard*, **a memoir of his service in**
     the Vietnam War

I Killed Sam

To connect with the author, please visit
www.robertsteadman.net.

Readers are encouraged to go to **www.MissionPointPress.com** to find information on how to buy this book in bulk at a discounted rate.

MISSION POINT PRESS

Published by Mission Point Press
2554 Chandler Rd.
Traverse City, MI 49696
(231) 421-9513
www.MissionPointPress.com

ISBN: 978-1-954786-52-3
Library of Congress Control Number: 2021918383

Printed in the United States of America

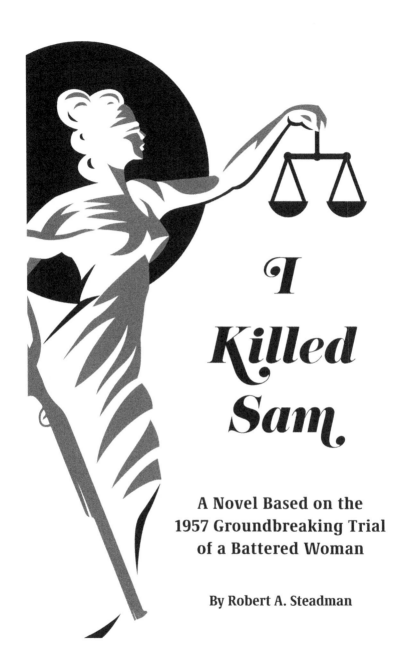

I Killed Sam.

A Novel Based on the
1957 Groundbreaking Trial
of a Battered Woman

By Robert A. Steadman

MISSION POINT PRESS

I dedicate this book to the three

most accomplished and intelligent women

I have known and loved unconditionally.

Bernice Trimble Steadman,

my wife

Calista Steadman Schwartz,

my sister

Calista Anne Steadman,

my mother

There is one universal truth, applicable to all countries, cultures and communities: violence against women is never acceptable, never excusable.

We must unite. Violence against women cannot be tolerated, in any form, in any context, in any circumstance, by any political leader or by any government.

Ban Ki-moon, former Secretary-General of the United Nations

Table of Contents

ACKNOWLEDGEMENTS

Working on this book, I found a coterie of great friends who joined to support me. First, of course, are my brother Dick and sister Calista, who were in my corner from the start. Pam Wakefield, a retired English teacher, corrected my grammar and punctuation. Lil Ostendorf, Meredith McComb and Theresa Lelito read and critiqued my efforts, all with pungent suggestions, and Ron Bohn gave unwavering support for me as a 93-year-old first author. Kevin Fitton did my initial editing and gave me a crash course in writing that added immeasurably to its quality. Grant Parsons, one of the finest trial attorneys I have been privileged to know, added tremendous suggestions, and Anne Stanton finished the editing beautifully, as only she could. She is my editor. I owe them all more than I can ever repay.

My brilliant mother and I loved murder mysteries, but my beloved wife, Bernice, called them "murder-mister baloneys." Regardless of this flaw, she managed to wind up in the Michigan Aviation Hall of Fame and the Michigan Women's Hall of Fame, and we enjoyed an extraordinary, loving marriage for fifty-seven years.

CHAPTER 1

"I Killed Sam"

It was a lovely fall day in **1987** and I was enjoying the warmth of the sun, leaning back on a comfortable chair on my deck overlooking the Flint River. I don't know why or where it came from this time, but I was again reliving the nightmare of Betty's life with Sam some thirty years ago.

Memory is tricky and extremely selective, blending the good and bad in less than equal shares. Mine focused on the incredibly terrifying, physical abuse of Betty, my gorgeous high school sweetheart, at the hands of a guy named Sam Waterman. He had brutalized her during the last three years of their marriage with the full knowledge and support of his dad, Ira.

Sam and Ira – their names are forever consigned to defining the ugliness that humans are capable of performing. Betty put an end to the abuse with a single shotgun blast, and my memory that day dwelled on the year of my life I gave to defend her.

The images were as clear as though it had happened yesterday.

It was Thursday, the fourth of October of 1956. I was reading the final brief in a case scheduled for trial when I heard the front door open and Stella, my secretary, greeting someone. I looked up as my office door opened and Betty, my high school sweetheart of more than ten years ago, stood there. She didn't step in, just stood there as though caught in time and unable to move. I had always loved her bright auburn hair and years ago had enjoyed running my fingers through it. My first thought was that it was the first time I had ever seen her look so disheveled. The picture of her framed in that doorway seemed strangely wrong.

Her green dress was gathered at the waist and fell all the way to her ankles, like a messed-up formal. It would have been attractive but it was wrinkled and hung on her like laundry, the wrong size. Stella hovered behind her, and I heard her tell Betty to go on in, but she still stood in the doorway, frozen after taking a couple of shuffling steps. Her face was a mess – bruises on the side of her face, clotted blood on her right cheek, a large purple bruise below a huge black eye. A trail of tears streaked through the blood from the corner of her eye down to her neck.

As I looked at Stella for a clue, she nudged Betty ahead, into my office. She took a few more steps and stopped again. She wouldn't look directly at me. Her eyes darted around the office like a frightened animal.

I slowly stood and broke the silence with, "Hello Betty, what can I do for you today?"

Of course, aside from that fancy diploma on the wall, there's another sort of diploma you get when you grow up in a small town. It's the degree you get from the University of Hometown. It didn't take a law degree to know it was Betty's bully husband who'd caused those injuries, and I was certain of it before she said it. It was infuriating because I'd known Sam Waterman as an ignorant ass who had lucked into marrying the sweetest girl in town without having the slightest notion of her intellect and goodness. It was a marriage that made no sense to me. I didn't like him, and the bruises and black eye I saw now amped what could only be called a native anger. Abuse of women was something bred out of me by a brilliant mother.

Betty finally looked me in the eye across my desk, took a long, shuddering breath and painfully sat down on one of the chairs at my desk like she was crossing a finishing line of a race, her entire body aching. She raised her swollen eye under that beautiful, auburn hair, and said, "I killed Sam." She repeated the words you never want to come out of anyone's mouth. "I killed him."

I started to ask, "Was it an accident?" but then stopped. I had been about to make an important mistake that could harm her. If there's a first commandment in a murder case, it's this: The lawyer doesn't want to know the ultimate answer. First, you have to know the story.

She continued shaking as she insisted, "My God, Bob, I just killed a man." Her anguish and words were palpable, but they weren't sensible coming from the most loving, warm and caring woman I'd ever known. I came around the desk, and she clutched my hand as I sat down beside her.

CHAPTER 2

Betty's Story

The legal profession's niceties, if you want to call it that, hold that a lawyer can't present a known falsehood in court but owes the client a zealous representation. In other words, lawyers invented "don't ask, don't tell" long before gays joined the military.

I had to know her story, but I had to know it without learning something that I couldn't directly contradict in court – that would be a lie.

I motioned to Stella. "Get your notebook, please."

"Betty, I'd like you to give me the basics," I said. "But I want you to let me direct the conversation. Do you understand me?"

She nodded but was still shaking as she began.

"Sam hit me harder than usual last night, then raped me with his shotgun."

It was the sort of statement that makes even a hardened lawyer look away. I had trained myself early not to do that. I watched her eyes for any telltale flutter. She didn't blink.

"After that, he grabbed my throat and told me he was going to kill me and Beth the next morning. He wanted me to know it and wanted me to know he'd found another woman who always gives him what he wants in bed. He said he was sick of me fighting him and Beth crying every time when he ..."

She paused, but when I nodded to prompt her to say it, she finished, "... hurts me."

I had to approach the issue carefully. "It seems incredible that he told you he was going to kill you and Beth. Did he say that? Did you really believe he actually intended it?" I asked. I was fishing for a "yes" and preparing to move beyond it fast, if necessary.

Her voice strengthened as she reacted to my question. I had gotten her off her internal track and was leading her, and she was following now.

"He's fanatical about what he calls 'his word,'" she said, making air quotations. "So, when he promises something, he'll keep his promise no matter how insane. He's always bragging about proving he keeps his word to his friends, even if it hurts him or he didn't really have to. There was no question in my mind. I knew he would kill us. This morning."

Now she looked desperately into my eyes, as if she were watching a film.

"We have an old-fashioned furnace with a wide door. He told me he'd stuff Beth in the furnace, just like he did Beth's kitten."

Once again, I was stunned by the cruelty of the image.

I led her through some more background, as I thought of how I could draw her out on the ultimate fact I needed. She quietly told me the story of her marriage: a litany of abuse, a psychopath's laundry list of rapes, beatings and threats for her and Beth.

I heard Stella snap her notepad, a sign I'd learned from experience that she was about to switch from note-taker to participant. Stella's a solid legal secretary, but her anger has a short fuse. She moved closer to Betty and grasped one of her hands.

The critical, touchy part for me – the shooting act – was coming. As she started to narrate that part, her head started to slowly shake back and forth as if she were denying her own words. Clearly what she'd done bothered her tremendously. I could live with that but only up to a point. That may be the toughest part of an attorney's job – shaping an unacceptable story in real time.

Some would call it making things up, changing the story, and maybe even lying. But that's not it at all. The church has its liturgy and so does the law, and the lawyer who's worth a damn is clergy in street clothes. The law is set up on archaisms and formalities that the average person can't possibly understand.

Choosing the right language for a criminal defense is maybe the only damn thing a lawyer really can do for a client. You explain what the legal words mean and what the meaning between the words mean before your client tells the truth the wrong way. That was the process we'd begun the moment she stood in the doorway to my office; I'd started leading her to the liturgy. Betty had the story, and the intensity of her answers coupled with her demeanor told me forcefully she had the truth, but I knew that wasn't enough.

She went on. "This morning I went into his bedroom to propose an agreement, but he seemed to be asleep. I reached under the bed for his shotgun, which was right where it always was, to make sure it wasn't within reach when he woke up angry. He was always angry. His anger has been as predictable as the sunrise.

"I remember thinking, as I slid the gun out from under the bed, how heavy, how cold it was in my hands. I stood there holding it, looking down at him. An image of his hands shoving Beth into the furnace washed through my mind and, in its wake, a scream inside my head, 'Oh God, no!'

"I must have pulled the trigger. I don't know how, and I can't say what actually happened. I have no memory of shooting him, just hearing that sound, then opening my eyes like in a dream and seeing a bloody mess on the bed."

I breathed a sigh of relief. I'd got the story out close to

clean. I needed to make a quick nip and tuck.

"So, he had promised last night to kill you this morning," I asked, starting the sequence.

"Yes."

"And he said he'd kill Beth like the kitten he'd burnt up," I said, knowing it was painful and wanting that.

"Yes."

"In that moment you heard something in your head," I said.

"Yes," and now she was crying, seeing the vision again.

"And you didn't say anything aloud? Was it all in your head?" I leaned a bit closer so she'd feel the pull of the story I was saying.

"No, I didn't say anything."

"So the words were a sound in your head. Something speaking to you, not you making words, just some sort of sound."

She was nodding.

"It was just a scream, like 'nooooooooo.'" I held my breath as she nodded, and then I repeated it.

"Noooooooooo," I said. "It was not about doing anything, it was just some panicked sound that took over in your brain."

She sobbed a long last time and then said, "Yes." The case clicked into place in my head.

She went on, talked about her powerful sense of guilt and shame despite all the abuse and threats and infanticide talk. Then she gave in, spent from the effort, stopped talking and crumpled sideways against Stella.

In that instant, my practice came to a screeching halt. It's hard to explain the adrenalin rush of knowing when a "cause" case drops on you, given that nothing perceptible happens in the moment. No one stirred except for Betty softly sobbing. But I felt the sort of adrenalin that floods and then pools and stays.

It came, I suppose, from knowing her and being bonded so completely to her own terror. I knew her. That was it. Her story was too much mine.

We'd grown up in the small town, been in the same grades in school, and dated our senior year in high school. Her story was such a part of mine that her risk was now gut-deep for me.

I'd known when I came back to our little town from college and the army that she'd married Sam Waterman. I knew it had been a big mistake but didn't let myself think past that. Sam was a zero in my book, a big offensive lineman who had cleared the way for me, a halfback on our high school football team. He was a guy stupid enough to believe he made the sun rise and set. When we won, he turned on the Big Man act. Then he'd sulk when I'd get the usual press coverage of touchdowns, and he'd only get the lineman's generic mention.

In school, he hadn't been shy about his opinion of me, and I'd returned the favor. We moved in different circles of friends, which in high school was as good as a no-contact order from a court. After I left Darien and would visit for a holiday, our drinking habits crossed paths but his crass jokes and yee-haws were like bug repellent across a barroom. I steered clear.

The part that always boomed loudest was the sexual conquest stuff. Stuff about abusing women, grabbing them, forcing them. Getting away with it. In a small town like Darien, everyone seems to have a theme, for better or worse. Sam Waterman was a braggart of a certain stripe, God's gift to women, sure everyone wanted to hear his latest sexual exploit, whether or not it was true. Well over six feet and 250 pounds, he'd matured from a muscled bully into a lumpy bully.

He bragged what his wife would do for him on command. He shifted his heft as he told his story for emphasis. There is a sense of violence and betrayal in that kind of story, in my estimation. A man telling profane tales on his own wife may be the ultimate dregs of humanity. That sort of story always reminded me of a trapped animal being fooled with and tortured for sport, for superiority's sake.

For Darien women – or any battered woman in Michigan for that matter – there wasn't much chance of an "out." Divorce was an almost impossible choice with the usual devastating economic results for the homemaker wife and the probable, and even more dangerous, assaults. So, he had her, and he loved telling his friends about it. A couple of times, catching his voice from the other side of the bar-room and knowing it was Betty he was slurring, I felt the urge to stand up and confront him. She didn't deserve that. But I just sat. I rationalized – she's not my wife and not my life.

But deeper down, I remembered. She had been my favorite, the brightest in our class, sincerely warm and with that auburn hair and those eyes. There came a point in high school when she'd blossomed, and I finally saw her for the first time, feeling that instant flush. All that year she was my girlfriend. We canoed, hiked, and inhaled each other. We dated like we were in a bubble.

But high school love can't compete with reality. We were both headed for college in different states and had dreams of advanced degrees. Sure enough, ways leading to ways, as they do, we lost touch a year or so after grad-uation. I happened onto a Brooklyn gal during my time at Wesleyan. When I came back to Detroit for my bachelor's degree and law school at Wayne University, I had no occa-sion – or whatever it's called when you're young and the future is all you can think about – to contact her again.

Marriage for me happened with someone else, and then the army, and that, as you could say, was that. When I moved back to Darien, after a three-year legal apprentice-ship in Flint, I knew she'd married Sam. And that again, as I look back, was that. Except, with an asterisk. I'm not the first man who ever looked back and wondered "what if," and I don't think such reflections, contrary to what Jimmy Carter thought of such things, are any sort of betrayal. Life happens, and it seems to remember you just as vividly as you remember it. You can pretend the past is past, but there's memory in your nerve endings.

I'd see her occasionally on my visits to Darien.

She'd kept that gorgeous hair at shoulder length and wore simple, long dresses that hugged her figure from head to toe.

A small town is a place where a smell or a whistle or a face in a passing car window tell a story more complete than any novel. Sam knew that Betty and I had been an item and didn't miss a chance to trot out his – what, his inadequacy, his insecurity, his jealousy? – every time he'd see me across the bar. If he noticed me in hearing distance, he'd put her down like someone heeling a dog, because he knew about us and wanted me to know what he did to her now.

Once or twice, I caught her eyes just before she looked away from me in his presence, and I could see what I thought was her embarrassment. I assumed she was thinking, "Yes, I know I made a mistake, but he's my life now."

When her life with him became a book opened in my office, I wished to God I had read it earlier.

CHAPTER 3

First Impressions

I'd got some elements from her that would make a case, and I knew some of the elements that would go into the story against Sam, so I was started. Still, though, there's the lawyer's axiom: Don't sniff your own fumes. If there's an ounce of doubt, it'll be exploited, so you might as well clear the air right at the start.

I remember my first impression of Betty's case was that there were no apparent viable defenses, except ... That's all I can say. Except. A guy got shot to death in bed, apparently defenseless at the moment, one of God's creatures bloodied and pockmarked with buckshot – not a pretty sight. Her account of his abuse would get her sympathy, but spouse abuse alone was not a legal defense. In the dark ages of the fifties in Michigan, husbands could abuse their wives in demanding their performance in the bedroom, meaning that sex with a wedding band wasn't rape regardless of any force the man used. The only brutalization of a wife that was criminal then was murder. The discrimination was virtually complete against her.

Regardless, there was no question about taking her case. I considered helping her as an old friend, and her account of Sam's abuse enraged me. After telling me her story, I told her she needed an attorney, and she asked if I would represent her. She assured me her parents could come up with a retainer. I didn't worry at that point about the costs even though my practice had already taught me it should be my first concern. I just told her I would, and that was that.

I was certain the prosecution would assume her case would be an easy victory. The probability was that they would spend only a little time in preparation, and if I could come up with some surprises, we might be able to move a jury away from first-degree murder. The county prosecutor, Jerry O'Bannon, and I were not friends, far from it. Our history would ensure that he would take every opportunity to denigrate me, and it was probably pure bravado to think I was her best answer against his greater experience and personal animus. But I knew no one would work harder for her and believed my skills were sufficient to handle him.

When you compare his perceptions and approach to trial to mine, the biggest difference was always his overwhelming desire to win at any cost. I had a young lawyer's bright-eyed faith in justice and fairness. A jury senses the difference, and it's a difference that packs a wallop in cases where the jury has room for sympathy. He cherished his trial record of victories and assigned most of the easiest cases to himself to perpetuate that apparent proof of his dynamic trial abilities. It was a virtual certainty he would handle Betty's case since it would be extensively publicized, and there was no obvious defense. I pictured him salivating at the chance to demonstrate his superiority to me. He would count on another victory for his trial record.

Everyone in our small town knew O'Bannon's political status, knew he'd sell his soul for continued prominence as a rising star in politics. He was a climber, a man running for something bigger, a prime example of the Peter Principle – rising to one's level of incompetence. I'd never fallen for his handshake and smile. He knew it. He knew because I let him know it. That's something good, young lawyers have – a disrespect for authority. If he ever actually got a job at the state level in the party, they would be getting a dud. But I really didn't give a rat's ass, as the beloved saying goes. I never did take to bullshit artists, and he was a manure spreader, par excellence.

CHAPTER 4

Old Times

Thirty years ago, when Betty announced that she had killed Sam, my life was in reasonably solid condition and moving along a good track. My finances were in fine shape, and I lived in a nice older home on the river about a mile upstream from Darien, surrounded by my lifetime friends.

I had snoozed my way through college until reaching law school where, for the first time, I had found a place for combat of the mind to replace the sports I had relied on for years to satisfy my love for competition. College football gave me the opportunity to compete, but this exposure to the law and trial courts was an eye-opener. I loved it and finished the degree of Juris Doctor by the age of twenty-two, even while working nights on the Ford River Rouge engine line.

Sure, it wasn't all hearts and roses. I had been divorced for almost two years. Annie was an engineer in Detroit, and we first met at some function at the law school where I was finishing my degree. She was bright as hell and already – after working only two years with U.S. Royal Tire – had a couple of patents on tire treads. We were an instant couple and married quickly since there was a chance I'd get drafted after I graduated. Sure enough, my deferment ran out, and I found myself forced into the ranks of the U.S. Army within a month of taking my bar exam. The hiatus in the army – close to three years – didn't help our marriage, and it turned out we had different lifestyle aspirations. I intended to work as a small-town lawyer, which wouldn't satisfy her own high-flying ambitions. I'll admit we both tried, but I was not as supportive as I should have been, and quite honestly, neither of us thought we could last.

After my army service ended, I came back to Michigan, where I worked for a year for a terrific attorney in Flint learning the ropes – legal strategies and tools they don't teach you in law school. I spent another year as an assistant prosecutor and then left to do trial work for another firm.

When Betty had walked in my office, I had been on my own for about two years and found it liberating to practice law without a boss – any bosses. Meanwhile, a personal injury case gave me a nice nest egg for setting up my practice for years to come.

Some lawyers might have coasted after that win, but I considered it a seed to grow my practice. I found a solid old building in the center of Darien, which had plenty of space for an expanding law practice. It had sat empty for almost six months, so I was able to snag it from the willing seller for less than its value. The ornate sign on the door, "Law Office of Robert Nichols," advertised the fanciest thing I'd ever aspired to occupying: the office of a small-town lawyer. With Darien a short drive to Flint, I had the best of both worlds.

I moved in the obligatory bookcases featuring impressive law books; a green leather couch rescued from a used furniture store; three matching and relatively comfortable leather chairs, also rescued; and an impressive old-fashioned solid walnut desk. I invested in an excellent leather attorney's chair for my office and installed wall-to-wall carpeting throughout. Stella and I set up a conference room with six chairs, a waiting room with four, and a sturdy table and a coffee maker.

The drip coffee maker was probably the most used item in our offices. Stella's office was next to my own, although I claimed the office with a big picture window, giving me a great view of Darien's main street. The other three walls sported my degrees and my single personal touch: a Winchester Model 50 shotgun hung on pegs. It was a proud possession I'd bought brand new when I got out of the army and customized with a top-grade poly choke. More than a few pheasants died in front of that gun.

I finished off a second office with a nice desk and matching chairs in case my practice grew. All in all, I considered it the most comfortable digs imaginable. I anticipated a lot of enjoyable hours in that soft, leather chair, never guessing what was coming.

I bought a lovely three-bedroom home from an older couple, whose health problems forced a foot-dragging move to Florida. My new house was on the river, but the water wasn't pristine in those days, polluted with farm fertilizers, massive quantities of manure, and just about anything else anyone wanted to throw in. In those days, people and companies brazenly dumped their garbage and waste into the river. Let's just say I never took my canoe out on hot, low-river days.

Almost simultaneously with buying the house, Flint entered into a joint development agreement with a Turkish city, and Annie applied to be our representative. She got the job and flew to Turkey where she met some teacher tourists from the UK. I wasn't too surprised when she called to tell me she had decided to stay in London with one of those teachers – a British man. So there I was. A not very proud divorced lawyer, feeling at least equally responsible for the final breakup. Then again, we both knew we never quite gelled after tying the knot.

Fortunately, my fledgling law practice was successful. There was substantial work and more importantly, I found I was pretty good in the courtroom although younger than most of my opponents. The years I had spent as an assistant prosecutor and working with the senior attorneys prepared me for my own solo practice.

It helped that I managed to recruit the senior attorneys' best legal secretary, Stella Anderson. She was my own age, married, with two small kids, and hands-down the best secretary I had ever worked with. When I invited her to come with me, she literally jumped at the chance and was with me from the moment I opened my rental office in Darien. It turned out she not only knew the legal system, she was also a decent human being. Truth be known, a great legal secretary is more "office" than any building. Stella was my cornerstone for the career I knew I wanted.

CHAPTER 5

Surrender

When we finished going over her story, I told Betty that we had no choice but to call the police.

"I'll start the process of your surrender. There's only one thing for you to remember – silence. You're the accused, and when the police say 'anything you say can be used against you,' it's true. Your life may depend on silence until we meet again."

I knew most of the police officers from my year as an assistant prosecutor. We'd worked together, formed some attachments. I could count on them to deal fairly with my client. My first call, though, while I still had Betty, was to Joe Flannigan, our local photographer. He came straight over. I needed good photos of Betty's bruises before they locked her up and the evidence faded.

The damage wasn't confined to her face. Her entire body was spotted with yellow, blue, and black bruises in various degrees of injury. I stepped out while Stella helped Betty undress. I could see on their faces when they emerged fifteen minutes later that Stella and Joe were both shaken by what they'd seen.

Joe promised a folder of color photos. Stella, usually my stoic rock, was near tears and embraced Betty protectively. She knew not to change Betty's appearance in any way before she could be examined. Even if she'd tried, all the makeup in the world couldn't conceal the massive bruise and black eye and the bleeding beneath it, which stood out like a neon sign.

Finally, I made the call. Sergeant Vince Brasso of the Michigan State Police, my best friend when I was an assistant prosecutor, came on the line. Reporting a death – maybe a murder – is not in the daily duty of a Darien attorney, but he reacted professionally. We arranged the surrender.

We met at Betty's home, at around 11:00 a.m. I didn't enter until they got there. Then I had only a minute to glance at the scene and make a few mental notes. Brasso's team took over efficiently and spent the next couple of hours cataloging everything and completing their forensics' exams.

The shotgun had done a complete job of obliterating Waterman. Since it was a crime scene, Vince couldn't let me get close, but I saw enough through the open door to understand why she was nearly unhinged when she arrived at my office. I wandered through the home and was struck by Sam's apparent disdain for her and Beth's comfort.

The place was a dump. Almost every room in the house was furnished with giveaway stuff from a flea market. Sam obviously was too cheap to spend anything to make it livable for his wife and child. With one exception. Sam's bedroom was the nicest room in the house, outfitted with top-of-the-line maple furniture and matching pillows and spread. It was opposite in every way from Betty's bedroom, bare of comforts except for the baby's crib her parents had given her and a sleeping cot.

The kitchen was a prime example of his neglect. The roof leaked badly, and there was water damage on the ceiling and the wall. The metal legs on the table and chairs were rusted, and the table marred so badly, it looked impossible to ever get clean. I sneaked a peek in the fridge, and there was damned little there, mirroring the paucity of canned goods and foods in the little pantry. I was getting madder as evidence of his lousy character mounted. Aside from the physical abuse, it was obvious he had tried every way he could to break her spirit.

After his first walk-through, Vince put Betty in his police car and permitted me to sit with her while they finished inspecting the home. At about noon, we noticed a blue Chevy approaching the front of the house with a woman driver. We couldn't get a good look at her, but we did catch the first three letters of her license plate – "HBV" – before she sped away. Betty thought it might be Sam's other woman, and I asked if she'd ever come to the house before. Betty was certain she had not, and we speculated a bit on what she was doing there that day. It seemed a strange coincidence but not important enough for a follow-up. I wrote down the first three letters of the license and made a note that it was a 1953 Chevy 210 two-door, just in case it might be useful down the road.

While at the home, I asked Vince to run a check on the residue of the furnace, thinking that evidence of the kitten's demise might show up. He didn't know why I asked but promised to see it was done. I pushed my luck a bit and asked Brasso if he knew of a good private investigator. I knew some, but I wanted a name Brasso might be friendly with.

"Crime scene or investigations?" he said.

"Nice if it were both," I said, thinking of the expense.

He gave me the name of Jim Drew, a retired state police crime scene investigator, who had been a top investigator before taking early retirement after a disabling road patrol injury. I knew the name but not his work.

Vince knew what I was thinking. "He's your guy," adding that he'd worked with Drew for some years. Drew had opened his office as a PI about six months ago. Vince jotted a phone number, ripped off the page, and handed it to me. "When you tell him where you got his name, tell him you're not sure," he said, and I nodded. Good advice.

If O'Bannon knew Brasso and I were friends, he would re-assign the case to someone else.

I had to turn Betty over to Brasso, step back, and let the police proceed. They read her the rights statement – out of deference to me they spoke in recognizable English – and she followed my instructions. Other than a vague assent when they asked her about the gun discharging and seeing my laser stare at her from a distance, she tiredly refused to say anything else.

When they were satisfied she was locked into her silence, they let me approach again. I told them we would cooperate in every way and would soon be willing to share her story. The younger cop with Brasso started to reply and then thought better. I couldn't blame him. It had to be frustrating, having a lawyer beat you to the scene of your murder case.

"I'll see you soon," I told Betty as they put her into the car again.

"Make sure about Beth," she managed to say before the tears started. She knew I'd already called her folks, Tom and Lucy, to arrange her care. They were Quakers. Tom had raised the question of the retainer, and I had to give it to him straight: $5,000. He said it was all he had and agreed. The misery of a parent whose child has been charged with murder – or would be soon – wrapped the whole miserable day in a sense of doom. There was nothing I could tell him to lessen the blow.

CHAPTER 6

Defending the Defenseless

I spent the next few hours in the office researching available defenses. It was an exercise in frustration. You can think of law as chess, and for every move there is a countermove. You need to plan the next move. And then the next. The problem for this case was the definition of self-defense itself. I needed to get Sam's abhorrent conduct before a jury. A claim of self-defense by Betty would make the abuse evidence relevant, but there was a problematic second element that required me to prove Betty had no chance of escape before resorting to lethal force. The court would have a basis for throwing out the abuse evidence if there was no realistic or reasonable belief there was, in fact, an *imminent* threat.

So, I had to prove she made the decision to shoot him for good reason, while also arguing that she didn't mean to do it. The added facts didn't help. Sam had apparently been asleep, defenseless, Beth safely in the other room, Betty free to leave or do anything she wanted.

I doubted there was a jury in the world that would

believe shooting Sam was her only way out. I could try to explain. Most all abuse victims stay silent, cover up bruises, and tell lies, better that than risk even worse injury of "normal" beatings. But I could only explain away so much. For three years, Betty had kept quiet about his violence. The idea that she had no other option than murder, as Sam laid quietly in bed, was the sort of stretch that a jury's sense of literal facts wouldn't bear.

The only real difference between a clever lawyer and a dullard lawyer is the facts. Good facts make good results. It's not quite that clear cut. But I can say, to a moral certainty, cleverness can be defined as preparation to present the facts in the best way. I needed preparation, and that would cost money.

When you prepare a murder case, you know it's unlikely your client will testify, so you have to be honest with yourself. You are your client's storyteller. You have to stare in the face of each juror listening to your story. Are they following, or are they frowning? When I envisioned the jury listening to me trying to tell them Betty acted in self-defense, I saw a blank wall of disbelief.

She had no medical records of prior injury. She had never filed a single police report of past abuse for the simple fact that she had feared the police would believe Sam over her and Sam would then hunt down both her and Beth.

I hit Stella's pager button on the phone. "We need to talk," I said.

She had a cup of coffee in one hand and her pad and pen in the other. She knew what I was going to say.

"What do you think I've got?" I asked.

"You first," she answered.

"I know it's there, but I can't get it going."

I laid it out fairly. "Betty killed him to save herself and Beth. Lethal force is justified if she reasonably believes there's an imminent and unavoidable danger of death or grave injury to her or another at the moment she shoots. But Sam was apparently asleep, defenseless. Why didn't she just leave – that's what I have to explain?" I looked at Stella, but she wasn't going to help until I'd worked through it some more. She took a sip of coffee and crossed her legs as if she was settling in.

"I need to convince the jury that leaving was not an option, that it would have been a step toward greater danger. There's a crack in the law there."

"An expert?" Stella asked. It was the right question. A lawyer can fill in some missing facts with academics. Studies of abused women show certain telltales signs, and I might use that.

I went on, "Then there's the problem with the word rape, the marital exception."

Now she interrupted. "Remember Sam, what he did," she said. "He did it with a shotgun."

"You're right, but the marital exception to rape exists across the country. It's not considered a criminal act for a husband to rape his wife. Betty denied him."

I shrugged apologetically as I went down the list.

"Biblical support for the husband's superior status in the home, his right to control her, wives as child-bearing chattel, the judge is going to instruct the jury, and ..."

I started standing up from my desk in frustration.

Stella raised the pad and motioned for me to sit. "The jury will see her face. They'll spot Sam as a psychotic abuser."

"There's that statement she made," I said starting over. "That thing about the voice in her head."

"You did a good job making that a sound," she said.

"A temporary insanity defense is a hard nut to crack, Stella. The old M'Naghten rule test. She can't understand what she did or was unable to distinguish right from wrong."

"It was a voice in her head, a sound, as she thought of Beth being pushed into the furnace. C'mon Robert!" said Stella, smacking the pad down so emphatically some of her remaining coffee slopped onto the floor.

"Jesus, Stella, I'm just trying it all on. Give me some slack before we lock in a mistake. What am I missing?"

"You're missing your anxiety that it's *Betty*, and she's not anonymous off the street. That's what you're missing," she said, and looked away. Personal life was a line Stella and I had never crossed before.

"I'm waiting," I said.

"It's Betty, so it's different for you. But it isn't really, and you have to get that settled in your head. I've never seen you paralyzed, and this isn't the time to be afraid of a case just because you can't accept the risk of losing. Don't get a god complex on us, Robert. Remember your favorite saying: K-I-S-S, Keep it simple stupid."

"Kiss," I said, and chuckled. It was the right icebreaker. "I owe you a beer," I said.

"You owe me an acquittal of the person who finally stopped that execrable son of a bitch," she said. She fixed her eyes on mine, and then relaxed and gave me a reassuring smile.

I kidded her. "What happened to not having a god complex? You take that away and then you make god-like demands," I said.

"Let's get going again," she said. All business.

"Okay," I thought for a second and then exhaled. "Michigan gives us irresistible impulse as part of the temporary insanity defense. The defendant is unable to control or resist her own impulse and commits a criminal act by reason of insanity."

She said, "You think the voice in her head?"

"That's what she said before anybody got involved. I think it's the truth. That gets us going, and that may do it. At the least it gives us a basis for including the abuse evidence and an argument for acquittal as opposed to a reduction to a lesser offense."

"Any plan B?" she asked.

The question jogged my thinking. The judge might allow two separate and distinctly different defenses. That was in my favor. However, even if the court went along with the double-defense approach, adoption of the insanity defense would potentially mark Betty as an opportunist in the jury's view. The prosecution would do its best to paint her as bright, competent, and lying. O'Bannon would argue the insanity defense was a gimmick, and the sneer on his face would remind the jury of every skeptical reaction they'd ever had to letting obviously guilty killers go free. He'd point to Betty's education and intelligence as proof she knew exactly what she was doing.

"Self-defense?" I said tentatively. "The threat he was going to kill her and Beth that morning?" I waited, but Stella didn't respond. She needed more.

"Tell me what you think about this part," I said. "Why did she do it this day? Why today? And why no attempt to hide it, no faking anything?" As I asked, I realized why. It was because Betty had insisted that Sam was going to kill Beth and her that morning, and she believed him and the inevitably of the killing.

"Is that the missing part?" she asked. The part that proves conclusively she was certain imminent harm was coming unless she acted in self-defense?

Good question, but my brain had deflected again to my feelings for Betty and how they would make the defense more difficult. I had to figure out how to quickly move past that for lack of any alternative. I couldn't unmake my past life.

The thought Stella had posed raised other concerns. Betty's potential imprisonment was bad enough for herself, but it would be catastrophic for Beth. The first possibility of parole would be fifteen years down the road. The absence of the mother would result in permanent emotional distress. I had to find a way.

"Shit," I finally said and buried my head in my hands. "I have to get some air."

CHAPTER 7

Jim Drew

It was two in the morning when I stumbled into bed and 7:00 a.m. when I woke from a fitful sleep. Feeling sleep-deprived, I was in the office by eight, and fifteen minutes later, I was on the phone with Jim Drew, the private investigator. We scheduled an 11:00 a.m. meeting in his office.

Meanwhile, I walked down to Darien's only restaurant for some breakfast. The place was buzzing with the news of Sam's demise and everyone there had an opinion to share. There was damn little support, at first, for Betty. The main take was that she must have suffered a mental breakdown to shoot him the way she did. The speculation on the effect of a short-distance shotgun blast was pretty descriptive.

But the conversation began to shift. "The murder was so bad that maybe he'd deserved it." And some liked me more than the prosecutor. When I told a few folks that I would be representing her, most of them wished me luck. There appeared very little support or friendship for Sam. My dismal assessment of Sam was shared by most of the folks who knew him.

I'd won the jump ball. After eating my eggs, I swung by the office, where Stella had prepared the paperwork for my formal attorney's appearance for Betty, which would assure no one could question Betty without me present.

While waiting to head to Drew's office, I stopped at the jail. The corrections officer let me into the catwalk outside Betty's cell. She was sitting on the thin, plastic mattress in her dull gray cell. I spoke to her through the bars. She was wearing suicide-proof scrubs and flops. Her face was drawn, and she stood up to meet me with a forced smile. She put her hand over my fingers on the bar, and I thought of her in my arms, then kicked myself free again. I gave her some information to hold her over. "My guess is the prosecutor will officially charge you with first-degree murder at some point today."

"Okay," she said.

Just that. Her smile faded, and she shrank back into herself. I had to get to Jim's office in the bank annex.

"It'll be okay." The thing you always say when you leave someone jailed or dying in a hospital bed.

When I got to his office Drew was there, seated at a desk facing the door. It was a small room with one desk for his secretary and another for himself. There was a small side room through another door, and it reminded me of a squalid interrogation room.

His secretary was an attractive young lady who projected a strong air of competence. When Drew rose to greet me, I was impressed with his size. He was well over six feet and his firm handshake left no doubt about his physical strength. More important to me was the fact that he looked me in the eye.

Brasso had filled me in on Jim. He was a superb athlete scouted by pro baseball, but he'd decided on a police career instead. Brasso shook his head in wonder. Still, Drew got on a fast track for promotion. He was smart and personable and rising fast until he was hit by a drunk driver while questioning a driver he'd stopped. Severe leg trauma and a limp forced him into early retirement. Fortunately, the insurance company for the drunk driver had settled, providing him the nut to launch his private investigation business. With his technical abilities and the equipment he was able to buy, he was on his way to establishing a big-city name in Flint.

Brasso had called ahead and told him I was a straight-shooter who needed an investigator on a capital case. After the barest of pleasantries, I went right to it.

"So, what do you hear, and what do you think about this Waterman deal?"

Jim gave me a recitation of the gossip version of the facts. He said what I wanted to hear: "There's some healthy suspicion about the victim, but of course, that's just the street talk. There's also a rumor that she admitted everything. If that's the case, is there really much I can even do?"

"Yeah, quite a bit," I said. "I'm just starting. But this case isn't as black and white as you think. This is an unusually sympathetic perp. I need a complete workup on Sam's and Betty's friends. See if you can find anything that either of them said publicly or privately about their relationship. We need to find someone who knew about Sam's abuse. And finally, see if you can find something on Sam's skill level with guns. How many did he own, what kind, that sort of thing?"

I asked Jim if he could get me the name of the best private lie detector operator available. Jim looked pleased.

"I thought there might not be much I could do," he said, "but it looks like we might have a decent shot at this. If there's anything out there to find that will help, I will find it."

I was impressed and asked Jim about his fee. Jim gave me his quote and asked for a retainer of a thousand. I wrote him a check on the spot and felt some hope for the first time.

"One more thing," he said. "I know some good ex-police officers who have worked part time for me on a case-by-case basis. Okay if I hire them to help me?"

"Sure," I said. "Whatever you need." If there was anything or anyone helpful out there, I came away believing he would find it.

CHAPTER 8

Dr. Rob Willoby

When I left Jim's office, I headed for a phone to call Dr. Rob Willoby, a psychologist and therapist with a stellar resume – he was also a good friend. The receptionist told me he was out for a short time, so I headed over in hopes he'd have time to discuss the case. I needed to have Betty assessed by a psychologist as soon as possible. The prosecution would have to allow a medical workup, and getting it done within a few days of the arrest would give it credibility. Having worked closely on a case with Rob, I knew he'd have enough common sense to appreciate the dichotomy of two defenses. He also was high on the empathy scale. His assessment of the reasonableness and strength of Betty's belief that Beth was going to be killed with no path of escape would be crucial, if positive.

When I got there, his office was closed for lunch, so I whiled away the time eating lunch at a nearby restaurant. Promptly at 1:00 p.m., I walked into his digs. His secretary was just finishing her own sandwich, and Rob had just walked in ahead of me. I asked whether he had a few minutes to chat, and luckily, he was able to shift another meeting. His office was just as I remembered it, designed for comfort with soft chairs and a working table rather than a desk.

He had read about the shooting in the morning paper. When I told him of my appearance for Betty, he expressed commiseration with the difficulty of the situation.

"Looks like an impossible defense," he said.

"I need your participation in this impossible defense," I said, "starting with evaluating Betty's psychological profile."

Rob could outline core personality traits and identify any disorders that might exist, whether from the trauma of the recent past with Sam or from anything else in her background. I needed to eliminate areas of attack by the prosecution or, at the least, minimize any potential attack.

I quickly told him the details I knew – the history, the continuous abuse, the shotgun, the intimidation and fear for her little girl, and finally, Sam's threat that he would kill them both in the morning. I could see Willoby becoming more intrigued moment by moment, and by the end of the narrative, he was on board as my forensic psychologist.

He started with advice.

"Robert, I'm picking up you have personal feelings about this one. You think it might be traumatic for you. Have you thought this entirely through? Can you handle the risk of losing?"

I didn't have an immediate answer and knew I shouldn't fabricate a false one. It was the second unsolicited warning and tipped me off to something important. I was giving away my bias in the way I told Betty's story. I needed to learn to hide my feelings better.

Willoby went on. "I won't fixate on this, and it's not going to be part of my analysis of the case. But, friend-to-friend, just watch it. The time may come when you have a plea offer that means jail time. If you turn down the deal, it'll mean a big risk. You'll be committed to keeping her out of prison.

"It's not building the case that will be the pinch, it'll be advising the person whether to accept less than perfect results. That'll mean swallowing some sort of bitter pill instead of risking everything. Could you do that? Could you counsel someone you have feelings for to do something that will hurt both of you and separate you for a long time?"

"I see her more as a client than as a very attractive woman," I fabricated.

He let me get away with it for the time being. He added a few more preliminary thoughts about the defense and offered a date for Betty's exam. I told him there was little chance that Jerry O'Bannon would offer any kind of plea deal in any event because this case looked like an easy win and a chance to work me over publicly.

"That may be true," he said, "but just remember that the depth of her physical and mental injuries could make it impossible for her to have a normal married life. When she comes to accept that reality, it could lead to severe depression.

"And, of course, facing the possibility of being separated from her daughter for decades could sink her into a very dark place. Her depression will be most difficult to handle while she sits in jail alone, waiting for the trial and thinking about Beth."

He added a few more preliminary thoughts about the defense, and I went back to my office to prepare a motion for a court order, allowing him access for psychological examinations and therapy. He had made his points pretty forcefully, and they increased my confusion about what I could expect over the next few months. The result of Rob's evaluation would be tremendously important to our defense.

I had used expert witnesses extensively in previous trials as a prosecutor and read studies examining their effectiveness and why jurors accepted or rejected their credibility. It was generally true that expert psychology witnesses were most believed when several factors existed: if they were from the same general community as the party examined; provided psychotherapy (in addition to the exam); had previously testified for both the prosecution and the defense in criminal cases; and were not paid outrageous fees for their testimony in the case. Regular fees paid for therapy were not a problem in the jurors' minds. The ability of the expert to talk at the jury's level of understanding in a narrative style and to avoid direct criticism of opposing experts was clearly important.

Fortunately, Rob met all my criteria. I knew he would charm the jury. As a witness, he always came across as a really nice guy. He insisted on testifying with minimum pay except for the therapy sessions for Betty, who needed help in dealing with what she had done and the circumstances we faced. I asked for his report as soon as possible since I knew the judge would be asking for the defense's position. Filing a short synopsis with Rob's report attached would show we had cooperated with the prosecution. It never hurts to be upfront with the trial judge, and I looked forward to trying the case before Circuit Court Judge Blevin. He was a sharp judge with a reputation for fairness. I wanted him in my corner, at least on procedure.

I also wanted to get out front of the prosecution as far as possible and as soon as possible. District Judge Price called the prosecutor's office and signed my order when there was no objection expressed. I included the court's permission for extended therapy in the order and indicated we had no objection to medical and psychological evaluations by the prosecution.

I was confident Betty would believe the evaluations and therapy were necessary and important for her and Beth. I thought it was a good idea to confirm my confidence – and I wouldn't mind seeing her again – so I headed for the jail.

CHAPTER 9

Meeting Again With Betty

It was a relief to see Betty again, our first extended time since she had surrendered to the police. I described the work we had done so far and talked with her about Rob and his task to develop her psychological profile. She instantly understood the need and looked forward to therapy, just as long as it also included Beth.

"Of course," I told her.

She applauded the program I had laid out for Jim Drew. She brought up the defense costs and worried her parents could fund only a small part of it.

"I will do everything necessary to help win the case, and you can pay when you're able."

I told her that I wouldn't charge interest, and she knew immediately I was figuring time in prison.

"I'll pay for it all," she said, "regardless of how long it takes."

I asked her about her college experience and was incredibly impressed by her having attended Michigan State on full scholarship and graduating as the top student in that huge university. She had been the top student in high school, but I never realized her intelligence bordered on genius. I was somewhat mesmerized by the sheer brilliance of her mind, and it was no surprise when she diffidently confirmed she had a photographic memory.

"So, I have to ask. Why did you marry Sam?"

It was a lousy question under the circumstances since it openly implied her decision had been a poor one. But given her brilliance, it frankly bothered me that she had wound up with such a boorish slob. I guess our high school romance gave me a proprietary sense, because when I thought of them together, it really pissed me off.

She told me a sad, predictable story.

"I was depressed over the cancer death of my best friend and got drunk for the first time in my life at the local bar," she said. "I met Sam at the bar and woke up to find myself in his bed, although I have no memory of how I got there. When I learned I was pregnant, I told Sam, and he told me he had loved me for years.

"He proposed to me to give the baby a father and said we could get a divorce if it didn't work out."

Sam had initially been attentive, but after two weeks of marriage, Betty realized he was a possessive jerk.

"I told him no more sex and asked for the divorce he promised. He told me it would all work out after our child was born, and we could talk about it then. In the meantime, he kept his hands off from me and seemed to look forward to the new baby.

"So, a week went by, and I figure he has started seeing someone else. It wasn't a one-time thing, but all the time. But I had no interest in knowing who it was since he finally stopped arguing with me about sex.

"After Beth's birth, it was as if a switch had been engaged. Sam became terribly abusive with constant threats to kill both me and Beth. It became obvious he hated the presence of the child. I was terrified, and my thoughts focused solely on protecting Beth."

She stopped talking and closed her eyes. "I can't talk a lot about what happened. It's so ugly, the things he did to me. I'm ashamed. But he later bragged that he drugged me at the bar and took me home to rape me."

I did everything I could think of to get her to disclose the horrors of the past. With the little she told me, it soon became obvious we would need a full medical workup. I asked about her regular doctor, Dr. Ben Deering, a longtime friend of mine in Darien. She was happy with Ben and wrote out a note, giving him authority to share her medical history with me. From the way she still gingerly sat down, not to mention the bruises and contusions, I was pretty certain she needed medical attention immediately. Ben would be thorough, and his report would almost surely amplify what she had managed to share already.

It had been a long session. I explained the law and leveled with her that this would be a challenging case to win and why. As I got up to leave, she came at me with questions impossible to answer.

"Are you really telling me that everything he did to me in these past three years of hell means nothing?" she asked. "That the law says it's perfectly fine to brutalize and rape your wife? That you can force a toddler to witness such ugly and unmentionable assaults on her mother?" She looked disgusted.

"It is obscene! The law cannot be so terribly wrong! What he did, over and over *must* be a crime."

I had to tell her again that spouse abuse and rape of a wife were not crimes in Michigan. This had to be one of my worst moments as an attorney.

"He was a criminal, but the law just hasn't caught up. We'll have the jury's sympathy, but we can't rely on sympathy as a legal defense."

She was clearly shaken and depressed. "This isn't just

about me, but all the women who are suffering, day after day. Where is the justice?"

I had no words to comfort her. As I silently sat next to Betty in the gray confines of her cell, I tried to ignore thoughts of her spending year after year in prison. I started spinning downward, too, when I recalled Rob telling me to cool it. His words of advice calmed me down.

Betty took my hand when I stood up to go. Her hand was warm, and she held on for a short time with a strength approaching desperation. Her fears came through that grip in spades.

"Bob," she said. "I feel terrible to have involved you in something so sordid. I know my defense is close to impossible. I see all that you are doing to organize the case despite there being so little hope. Saying thank you doesn't begin to express how much I appreciate who you are and what you are to me."

CHAPTER 10

Ben Deering

A s I left her cell, I couldn't deny the electricity between us. I also knew the odds of her going to prison were overwhelming.

I called Ben as soon as I hit my office, and he was eager to help. I told him about my last talk with Betty and the note authorizing him to share her history with me. I needed a medical exam as soon as possible and suggested he coordinate his efforts with Rob Willoby.

"Sure, I can do it, Bob, but this is appalling," he said. "I haven't seen her in a long time. She's come in maybe once or twice since Beth's birth and then only to get help with insomnia. Of course, she must have been avoiding an exam to keep Sam's abuse a secret. I'll call Rob and schedule an exam with Betty right away."

I stopped by his office with a copy of the order and headed for home, exhausted. Checking my phone answering service, I found a call from Stella. In a tight voice, she told me I had missed several meetings and at least one deadline in court. She needed some direction and needed it now. In just a few days I had managed to outrage two clients and a judge. I didn't know what to do and realized for the first time how totally engrossing Betty's defense had become. I'd neglected my practice and had to figure out how to keep both trains on the rails – or crash.

CHAPTER 11

Canoeing the Betsie

With Betty's defense team put together, I spent a day in the office trying to get caught up. The clients were clearly concerned that I was too distracted with Betty to give them the attention they deserved and needed. I worked well into the night and all of the next day but still couldn't catch up. On the third day, I woke up tired and trying to figure out how to keep my practice alive and still obsessing about Betty's defense.

It was a particularly nice October day – the temperature in the sixties and no wind. I decided to take a day off to clear my head. I felt guilty leaving the mess for Stella but my love for canoeing won out.

Unfortunately, it was a low-river day, meaning the river outside my door smelled to high heaven. I decided to drive to the Betsie River, a few hours north, where I could rent a canoe and float without having to take my heavier Old Town with me.

When I pulled into the canoe livery, the parking lot was nearly empty. I saw only one other canoe on the river. As

I paddled, the Betsie was alive around me – deer on their beds along the bank, geese and ducks flushing ahead of me, the woodland sounds of honking and calling. I had dressed warmly for the river and the drift was just right. It reminded me of the paddling trips Betty and I had shared that one unforgettable year.

Her case kept encroaching on my thoughts, and the longer I paddled, the more focused the trial scenarios became. My research had made me face the fact that the case I was planning had never before succeeded – or at least it had never been reported in any of the Michigan precedents.

There was good reason for that. Combining a claim of self-defense and irresistible impulse weren't consistent logically or legally. Self-defense meant you acted intentionally because of a need to save yourself; irresistible impulse meant you acted unintentionally without any control over your actions.

If the judge allowed me to use both claims, I'd have to figure a way to get the jury to make a big jump of logic between the inconsistent claims.

First, to argue self-defense, I needed to get the jury to understand and believe Betty had good cause to fear that Sam would kill Beth the next morning. She had to convince them there was no way for the two of them to escape. Two long leaps of faith for the jury.

Maybe too long. I couldn't rely on self-defense alone. I needed a safety net under the self-defense claim, and that was where irresistible impulse came in. If I could develop a strong narrative of exactly what was going through her head when she pulled the trigger, I could give the jury a second legal reason to find her not guilty.

The idea was to make the jury see themselves in Betty's extreme circumstances, then put the gun in their hands and ask them what they would do with it.

Like an old defense pro once said, "Did the victim deserve to die, and was your client the one for the job?"

Even if spouse abuse wasn't a permissible legal defense,

I was going to use it anyway but call it something else. I wondered whether O'Bannon would find a way to object and block it.

Then again, it would take a tough judge to deny a murder defendant the opportunity to frame her case as she wanted. I floated on down the river, leaving the issue of the judge in the bubble line behind the canoe.

The strength of the case was the truth. Betty would have the burden of convincing jurors she was telling the absolute truth. If she made a single questionable statement, they would doubt everything else, and we'd lose the case. If they believed her, the jury would want to help her, and the final decision would be in their hands.

By the time I reached the canoe landing, the defense strategy was settled. I drove back to the office clear-headed and in a lighter frame of mind. Even the stack of work that greeted me as I slumped into my desk chair didn't completely ruin the feeling.

CHAPTER 12

Trial
Experience

In 1956, I wasn't a neophyte in the courtroom. My year in the prosecutor's office had confirmed that. I learned a lot about winning trials, but also the vagaries of office politics. To put it bluntly, I didn't get along with the chief prosecutor, Jerry O'Bannon, a relatively young wannabe firebrand whose political success was tied to his father's leadership in the General Motors strike and the formation of the auto workers' union in Flint. He was a publicity-directed Democrat and featured his father's activities as proof of his own abilities.

I had finished that first year in practice in an attorney's office and was recommended to him as an assistant prosecutor. He offered me the position, and I eagerly accepted. I knew the trial experience gained would be invaluable.

Pilots track their experience by hours in the cockpit. Lawyers track their experience in cases. In truth, most lawyers don't try cases; they settle cases. The difference is palpable, if you know what to look and listen for.

My year in the prosecutor's office taught me a lot of law

and trial work. It got me past the nervous, quavering voice, and it got me past the notion that I had to pull a rabbit out of the hat. It got me to the point where I knew if I prepared a case and looked a jury in the eye, they'd see what I saw. There was power in being able to relax standing in front of a jury staring at you.

There was another thing about that year under O'Bannon. It left me with a contempt for office politics and a specific contempt for the man himself. Jerry O'Bannon thought of himself as a rising star. In fact, his political success was the tail of a star, "connected" because of his father's leadership in the Flint GM strike and the auto workers' union. The name O'Bannon meant something in the region not because of the younger man but because of the older. Yet like most silver-spoon kids, Jerry didn't understand that. He sniffed his own fumes.

Before Jerry hired me, I'd had a year in practice with an attorney who recommended me to the newly elected prosecutor. When he called to offer me the job, I knew I needed to get out of the safety of the office and into the live combat of the courtroom.

The assistant prosecutor job called for trying cases in the circuit court and would usually require handling five or six cases during each jury term. I loved it and got pretty good at it. In fact, I wound up trying and winning seven major cases in a row during the fall of that first year with several of them assumed to be sure losses. In terms of attorney age, I was young, but in terms of courtroom experience, not so much.

....

O'Bannon called me into his office that December and fired me on the spot. "You're not doing your job," he growled, without looking me in the eye.

I looked at him in disbelief. "What have I done wrong?"

He pursed his lips, obviously hunting for a reply. "Well,"

he finally said, "I don't like the way you work with the other assistants."

We both knew the truth was that I wasn't doing the "job" of being an invisible underling. The truth was, I was actually doing a great "job" by winning tough cases and getting quoted in the news, and getting invited to speak to civic groups.

O'Bannon was a vain political climber, pure and simple, and the last thing he wanted was a potential rival the next time the prosecutor position was up for election.

I could have told him I'd never run against him. Running for office was my idea of dying and going to bureaucratic hell. But I didn't say that, because I wasn't going to lower myself to try to appease him.

I didn't pick my words. I just let 'em fly.

"Jerry, you're a talentless prick, and you always will be. You can't fire me because I just quit."

Later that day, I called an older attorney friend who hired me on the spot for more money than I'd ever made. He and his partner had one of the best divorce practices in town, but neither of them enjoyed trial work. He said that was going to be my main focus – trials – exactly what I'd figured when I made the call. The divorce firm experience went well and ended well, and we later parted friends. I had landed that big personal injury case, and the divorce attorneys had seen my passion was elsewhere. They blessed my departure honorably.

A year of working with Jerry gave me insights for Betty's trial. He was a counterpuncher who responded automatically and immediately to every action by an opponent. I always thought that if someone opened a window, he would reflexively jump through it. But he was also a cheat, a game player with evidence. I knew he'd refuse to share any information about Betty's case with me. My job was to determine how to leverage his practice proclivities – impulsivity on one hand and deception on the other – to my benefit. I knew I could bait him into anger.

I saw my chance at payback after Betty's preliminary examination – a hearing which is held in Michigan's felony cases to determine whether there is sufficient proof to bind the defendant over to circuit court for trial. It is normally just a pro forma exercise where the defense gets a chance to cross-examine the prosecution witnesses. But it usually features only one witness – the policeman heading the investigation. His testimony is almost always taken from a universal script employed by the police. If you've heard one police witness, you've heard them all. There was one thing for sure. There would be no surprises in Betty's preliminary exam since she had already admitted to the shooting.

After the prelim, I walked into the small, adjacent attorneys' room and noticed a several-page document lying on a desk. To my surprise, it was a copy of the prosecution's investigation report for Betty's case, listing witnesses, theories and other examination results. In federal court, the prosecution must share the report with the defense, but back in 1956 there was no Michigan court rule that required sharing. Most prosecutors did it anyway, and I did too, believing that the prosecution had a sworn duty to ensure justice for all citizens of the county, including anyone charged with a criminal offense.

O'Bannon was one of the few who flat-out refused, and no one had ever called him out on it. I thought about it for a moment or two and then took a quick look at the report. It was obviously a simple recitation of Betty's story and nothing else, so I took it next door, made a copy, and returned the original to that empty room.

I knew Jerry would be mad as hell if he knew I had the report, even though it offered nothing of interest. If there had been, I would have left it unread after my initial scan. But there was a major takeaway – the prosecution considered the case a slam dunk. Betty shot Sam, end of story. Jerry's examination of John Stevens, the lead police investigator, confirmed the investigation had gone no deeper. With Jerry viewing the case a surefire winner, he had decided to try the case himself. A perfect chance to add another feather to his trial headdress and lead the war dance around the fire. Having me as the sacrificial goat must have appealed to him as well.

I wasn't yet sure how, but I thought there was a way the report could be leveraged during trial. A real chance to ring his bell. I wanted him so angry that he would try to bulldoze Betty and, hopefully, make a major misstep or build some sympathy for her in the jury. Who knew? But at least I could have some fun. Until that moment, I wouldn't have known how to describe my strategy in words, but I knew now there was a necessary element in my case. I needed an angry, overreaching, offensive public prosecutor. Jerry fit that bill.

"And now," I said under my breath, "you have a way to make that happen."

CHAPTER 13

Gun Examination

I **needed to lock down evidence** of Sam's incredibly abusive treatment of Betty. I contacted a local lab that specialized in the investigation of biologic evidence, and based on what I told them I wanted, they told me what they needed.

I prepared a short motion for a court order allowing a forensic examination of the murder weapon. I kept it simple, you might say deceptively so. My motion requested the gun be produced for two hours to my qualified forensic lab, which would run nondestructive tests. The evidence would be preserved intact. There was nothing specific about it. O'Bannon, on cruise control, did not object, so Judge Price signed it quickly the same day.

On the day set for the exam, John Stevens, the state policeman in charge of the prosecution case, took the shotgun to the lab and remained within sight of the gun in the lab room while the exam took place. Shawn Roberts conducted the tests I had requested and when completed, Stevens left with the gun.

The lab furnished me with Shawn's curriculum vitae and it was excellent. He qualified easily as an expert in his field, and the lab assured me he would be available for trial. The lab's test results were available the next day and confirmed Betty's claims completely.

The gun examination was a major piece of evidence that supported her story, but one that was hard to stomach. It confirmed one of the worst actions of physical abuse imaginable. The report was clear that her future ability to someday have a normal emotional and physical relationship could be permanently damaged by his brutal and horrific assaults on her.

I remembered I had made a dinner date that night with a lovely lady friend who was just returning from a vacation in the south. Marilyn and I had spent a lot of time together since my divorce, and she was fun, sexy, always filling me up with compliments. Neither of us considered it a long-term relationship, but we had good times and I looked forward to seeing her again. It had been at least three weeks since our last meal together. I called to confirm I would be picking her up at six and looked forward to a good steak and conversation. Sure enough, it was a lovely get-together, although I found myself thinking of Betty through the entire evening. I walked to the counter to pay the bill, and unfortunately, I was interrupted by an irate client. The gist of his grief was his belief that I had abandoned him and my other clients to defend a killer. He rode his complaint horse up one side of me and down the other. He left me there with a simple statement: "Get your damn work done or forget any further business from me."

Marilyn had seen most of this and was intrigued at the mention of Betty. It was the first time she'd expressed any interest in my private life and suddenly suggested she might be ready to pursue a potential relationship. I deflected, saying I was too busy now with my defense of a gal who had killed her husband. I left it at that. From my perspective, it was an area I was unwilling to discuss. On the drive to her home, I detected a bit of coolness, and it didn't bother me. Betty had become more than a client, and I felt some sort of loyalty to her. It was obvious Marilyn wasn't in the cards for me, but I couldn't move in Betty's direction either, at least not yet under the circumstances. First, I needed to keep her out of prison.

CHAPTER 14

Scheduling Conference

Circuit Court Judge Sol Blevin called a scheduling conference for the first week of November. He wanted to hear our take on the trial and what motions would be coming up. I had prepared a short brief setting forth in broad terms Betty's claims of abuse leading to her belief that Sam was going to kill Beth on the morning of the day when she shot him. I attached Rob's preliminary psychological examination report, which confirmed his belief that she was telling the truth. He called it self-defense without question. You can't introduce an expert to opine whether someone's telling the truth, but you certainly can retain a cognitive testing expert to say a person gave truthful answers to his questions – and then repeat the questions he asked. The law of evidence requires more than a little hairsplitting. In Betty's case, I knew how to split them.

The report went on to state that, given the level of psychological injury Betty demonstrated during the testing, her momentary actions during the incident were most likely the result of an irresistible impulse based on fear. He believed, to a reasonable degree of psychological science, Betty had been temporarily insane at the moment the gun went off.

He stressed "at the moment the gun went off" instead of saying "at the moment she pulled the trigger."

I told Judge Blevin we would be offering his final report as a defense exhibit at trial and intended to argue both defenses – self-defense and irresistible impulse – since each had its own basis and each supported justifiable homicide. I had also attached my legal research citing court precedents allowing me to use multiple defenses. Jerry actually jumped out of his chair as he objected, but Judge Blevin cut him off.

"What is your legal objection?" he asked. "The defense has a right to argue as many defenses as it pleases, and justice demands we listen before striking any that present no factual basis. Mr. O'Bannon, have there been discussions regarding possible plea deals in this case? There was significant abuse of this defendant that could support charging her with a lesser offense."

"Absolutely not, Judge," he said, turning to sneer at me. "She blew his head off with a shotgun and no offer will be made of a plea deal. These purported defenses are ridiculous on their face."

He had made his position plain. There would be no quarter given. Judge Blevin appeared surprised at Jerry's apparent anger but calmly went on.

"How many experts will each of you be calling?"

I gave him the name of Shawn Roberts as my gun expert, Rob Willoby as my psychologist, and Jim Drew as my investigator. Also, we would call officer John Stevens and Dr. Ben Deering, who had conducted the medical exam. I agreed to file a list of additional witnesses within sixty days and Jerry was told to do the same. We would be given another fifteen days after the opponent's witness list was filed to add other witnesses, including any rebuttal witnesses. Judge Blevin set a trial date of Monday, February 4, 1957, and we were done. As Jerry stormed out, angrier than I expected, I wondered if there was a negative history between them, too.

I was thrilled that there would be no question regarding use of both defenses, although my brief in support had been solidly based on case law. Presenting multiple defenses had strong support legally, although the joinder of self-defense and irresistible impulse had never been attempted. I had concluded they would work seamlessly together.

Jerry's reaction to the defense's reliance on two different theories told me he thought I was desperate. He was certain the case was a sure thing, meaning he'd relax rather than do serious pretrial work, which gave me hope. I was also counting on the certainty that he'd rely on the marital exception law, which said a husband had the legal right to rape his wife without facing criminal charges. I thought the women on the jury would be surprised, shocked and angry to hear they were second-class citizens.

Based on my year working for Jerry in the prosecutor's office, I believed he not only would argue the marital exception, he really believed it was good law. His views of women were old-fashioned at best and demeaning at worst. His mindset on this was a potential minefield for him that he wouldn't see coming. He would be cocksure the men on the jury would be with him and relatively unconcerned about the deep-seated feelings of the women. The harder he hammered away at the right to rape, the better my chances to split the jury at a minimum. Jerry was in for a donnybrook. If I could stoke the women's anger at the law's discrimination, while creating empathy for Betty who had suffered vicious abuse for three years and ultimately would do anything to save the life of her child, I might just defeat the first-degree murder charge and the life sentence.

It was a neat and clean conference, but, when O'Bannon stormed out, angry, as if the judge had given him a bad shake, I gave Blevin a brief look of "what's that about," as if I didn't understand O'Bannon. The judge returned the smallest wink. You call that a clean kill at the pretrial stage.

Both of my defense theories were accepted, my best evidence was going to come in, and the presiding judge was starting with a clear idea of who was the bad guy and who was the good guy, at least as far as the lawyering went. I'd set a good foundation for Betty.

O'Bannon's angry reaction told me he was high on his own fumes. I wondered how many married women we would seat on the jury and how they would react to O'Bannon's insistence that marital rape was legal.

I recalled my father's approach to debate. He was the first from a farm family in South Dakota to go to college and earned a doctorate in political science from the University of Chicago. A brilliant debater, he once told me that to win, you need to turn your opponent's strongest point against him. I planned to. I was working on O'Bannon's angry certainty of a win, and my work was producing results. I needed just one juror to acquit. O'Bannon needed all twelve.

CHAPTER 15

Jim Drew's First Report

A **few weeks had passed** before Jim Drew met me to review the preliminary report.

"What did you get?" I asked.

"Some of them talked," he said. "Three of Sam's buddies talked on record about how Sam constantly bragged about how he abused Betty both physically and sexually, and how he controlled her every move. They said he talked in detail about how he knocked her around and called little Beth 'the brat.' They're willing to testify he openly made threats of violence against both Betty and Beth."

"Willingly?" I asked.

"Well, you know," he replied with a smile. "I mentioned the shotgun rape and the furnace, and they gave him up."

I shook my head in wonder. "You're the best." Getting a dead man's friends to turn on him was not work for an amateur.

"Not only that, but how about this for irony – Waterman taught gun safety through the local NRA."

"You mean these guys knew he was raping her with the gun?"

"Yes, after I reminded them. It's pretty obvious where he learned how to abuse his wife. I interviewed Sam's old man, Ira Waterman, and it's clear that house was a powder keg of tension. While I was there, his mother, Evelyn, acted like a hurt dog on a leash, didn't say a word. He actually called her a bitch in my presence. She has multiple scars, old and new bruises, and a look in her eye that is literally wounded. I watched her out of the corner of my eye, sitting scrunched over in silence, while the old man told me how Sam was so much better than that bitch Betty he married."

Drew let out a deep breath.

"The guy is so stupid I actually have him on tape saying he expected Sam to finish her off." He stopped for effect.

"You what?" I almost yelled.

Drew nodded and went on. "He was more amazed than sad – it was weird to listen to him. He was angry she'd killed Sam, rather than him killing her. I didn't include it in my report because it was just a feeling, not something you could rely on, but that old man sounded to me like he was faulting his son for not killing her first."

Drew looked at me with something like wonder.

He went on.

"He told me Sam should have gotten rid of her and married another woman named Elsa. He said Sam didn't divorce her because it would make him look bad in town. If he turned her loose, he knew she had friends who'd believe what she said about him, and he'd have trouble replacing her. He said that – 'replace her' – like he was talking about a farm animal."

I had to ask, even though it was irrelevant to the case.

"Sam hated me as much as he hated Betty. Did the old man mention any of that?"

Drew nodded. "He said Sam knew when you moved back to town. He knew if you heard him talking about her it would piss you off. He played you by hurting her even worse."

I couldn't stop a reflexive groan.

"She begged him for a divorce, but Ira said he didn't want to give you the satisfaction. The old man told me Sam would 'use her up' before he finished with her. That's in my notes, believe it or not."

It was what I'd been after, but it didn't feel good getting it confirmed. I couldn't erase the picture forming in my mind of the years of mistreatment she'd suffered.

"Robert, I'm telling you something that Ira said, and I quote: 'Sam would give her a taste of his shotgun in her along with a promise to belt the brat, and that would be all it took to make her shut up.' He was so proud of the son of a bitch he'd fathered and trained that he couldn't stop talking."

"Anything else," I asked.

Drew had interviewed Betty's parents, Tom and Lucy Morse, and the contrast could not have been more striking.

"They're devastated," he said. "They knew Betty had been unhappy but had no idea how traumatic her life was or the danger the child was in. It was beyond their comprehension as Quakers."

Beth was now with her grandparents and was a beautiful child, he reported.

"Go figure," he shook his head.

"Betty's extraordinary," I said. He understood what I meant.

Drew had also turned up a surprising number of witnesses willing to vouch for Betty's honesty.

"The best one might be the local banker who knows her reputation and her old boss at the bank. I can give you a list of another five or six willing to testify about specific instances who meet the criteria."

Drew was anticipating the hearsay and reputation challenges I'd have to counter. Reputation witnesses cannot testify about their personal opinion of a person's honesty, but can testify to specific instances concerning a person's personal integrity.

O'Bannon's temperament and certainty would lead him

astray. He would be lazy and make the mistake of opening the door and make Betty's honesty an issue, and I would drive a Mack truck loaded with reputation witnesses right through it. It was almost certain that Jerry would challenge Betty's account of Sam's abuse and his threat to kill her and Beth. I was confident our reputation witnesses could rebut his challenge. Another piece of the case clicked into place.

It continued to come down to whether Betty could convince the jury she was totally truthful. Truth would be our ultimate defense.

Assuming Jerry used Dr. Arti Brown to tell the jury she was lying, and he came to the trial ill-prepared in his usual fashion, we had to be ready for him. I told Jim we needed a complete workup on Dr. Brown with particular emphasis on his record as an expert witness over the past three years. He had been a favorite of Jerry's and my estimate of him was that he was full of himself and vulnerable to an effective cross-exam.

CHAPTER 16

Elsa, the Other Woman

Before parting ways, Jim told me the story of Elsa Howard. She had moved to our city about four years ago, and she and Sam had been an item before his get-together with Betty. In fact, Sam had recently proposed, and she was looking forward to their marriage.

Jim had talked with her at some length and found her deeply angered and nursing a visceral hatred for Betty. She gave every sign that she loved Sam and didn't believe that he had done anything wrong that would justify Betty's shooting him. Sam had showered her with gifts and the Spartan condition of his home demonstrated where all his money went.

Elsa believed to the core that Betty was a murderer – a killer who had taken her man from her. She told Jim that Sam had promised her he was going to "clean house" after the kid was born, and he would marry her then. She claimed he never mentioned divorce, but didn't explain what he meant by "cleaning house." But she told Jim, she was sure he would do it since she found him to always be true to his word. She had told Jim proudly: "My man always tells me and everyone else the truth. He never had any secrets from me, and we planned a future together."

When Jim had asked her again about the cleaning house reference, she blew him off.

"That was his business, not yours," she said.

The depth of her hatred was so extreme, Jim believed she was over the edge and potentially dangerous. His police training kicked in, and he followed up with a background check. He found her record in Kent County where she had been charged with involuntary manslaughter in the deaths of three small children in a day-care facility where she had worked. She was found not guilty in a jury trial.

Jim's fellow officers told him they were still angry about the case – she was guilty as hell, but there just wasn't enough evidence to convict her. They said her violent temper and abnormal behavior during the trial led to serious questions about her mental condition. A police psychologist had diagnosed her with incipient schizophrenia, although there was no formal examination available backing his speculative diagnosis.

Jim did a deep dive into Elsa's schizophrenic tendencies and found that those with the disease were more likely to behave violently. So, there it was. Elsa and Sam. A coupling from hell. Her lack of empathy for children led to their deaths in a day-care facility. And then there was Sam, who despised Beth solely because she got in the way of his sex life. Although there seemed no reason to use Elsa as a witness – there was no apparent evidence linking her with Sam's abuse – we would be ready if the prosecution tried using her as a witness for any reason.

"Jim, I want her served with a subpoena to make sure she's available if the testimony in the trial brings her into the mix. I think Betty will be okay – at least Elsa won't be able to get to her while she's in jail."

Jim's tapes were a gold mine supporting Betty's story, and my trial strategy was getting stronger. But we were still struggling with the same key problem in our argument – that Betty didn't choose to flee the scene.

I still thought a lie detector test would be a useful item in my back pocket, although the rules of evidence did not permit them to be introduced at trial. It was a usual ploy for the prosecutor to offer a lie detector test. A refusal to take the test could be used against the defendant, implying guilt. If the prosecutor tried that with me, I wanted to be able to answer with results from a reputable firm.

Jim had lined up Mark Givens, the top private expert in the state. Mark's stellar reputation was based on the quantity and quality of the testing he performed for various employers, as well as for several high-profile criminal trials where his testing was allowed into evidence for reasons that would not allow it in our case.

Under the guise of further psychological evaluation, Mark tested Betty. She passed with flying colors, and his report to me was complete and uncontestable. Everything she had told me was true. It may seem a little ridiculous to have had Betty tested, but one of the first important lessons I had learned as a trial attorney was not to assume your client is telling the truth or disclosing everything, including facts that would hurt his or her case.

I had believed Betty from the first moment she confided her story, but I also had picked up her anger. I was honestly relieved to have this confirmation of her truthfulness. At the same time, it was all the more reason to fear mistakes on my part. I just had to win for her. She was innocent.

CHAPTER 17

Defense Witnesses

I filed our witness list with the court well before the deadline Judge Blevin had established. I assumed Jerry would be filing his within a day or two of the deadline. I expected few, if any, surprises. We would have fifteen days after his filing to add any new witnesses we needed for rebuttal. Even before Jerry's filing, our witness list was growing. There were several keys to our defense and a number, including the reputation witnesses that I hoped would not be necessary.

Stella prepared subpoenas for them now that we had a trial date. I had once watched an opponent lose his case because his witness had been subpoenaed too close to the trial date. Unfortunately for him, his witness was on an extended vacation and couldn't be served. Aside from the fact that early subpoenas give the witness time to plan on the date, it always makes sense to work with your witnesses. Turning them against you can cause a huge pain in the ass.

When Jerry called regarding the witness lists, I asked

who would be doing the workups. Sure enough, he named Dr. Arti Brown, the local psychiatrist who testified in numerous cases for Jerry. He was known as a whore in O'Bannon's stable, a poor excuse for an expert. But he'd say what O'Bannon told him to say.

Jerry's primary avenue of attack was by surprise. He favored pulling a rabbit from the hat as a demonstration of his trial expertise. A fan of combat myself, I had no compunction against responding in kind.

While Jerry would engage in legal rhetoric, I had the physical evidence of the remains of a kitten in the furnace found by the state police and the obscene, physical proof of vicious, multiple rapes and blows. I would be laying the groundwork for the jury to acquit and would be hoping our evidence would be so strong it would support legal justification for that verdict. I first needed to make the jury want to find a path to a "not guilty" verdict, and then I'd have to show them the legal path to get there. That was my ultimate job.

If anyone had asked whether I was hopeful, my answer would have been ambiguous at best. As a former prosecutor, I was pretty sure the slam-dunk approach would be tough to beat. I could count on the jury being overwhelmingly sympathetic, but that didn't change the fact she had shot him while he was fast asleep.

Law Practice in Trouble

I **realized the case had usurped my life,** leaving a number of matters that needed work in my law office. Stella was doing her best, but the grumbling had reached a fever pitch. My practice was falling apart with clients calling daily, demanding to know what in hell was happening. Betty's case had the potential to ruin my law practice, and Stella was beside herself trying to keep our clients satisfied.

The reality of the problem was brought home to me when Jesse Hampton, one of my most important commercial clients and a very good, longtime friend, found me eating lunch at my favorite diner in the city. He sat down and called the waitress over to order. Then he really unloaded on me.

"Dammit, Bob, what in hell are you doing to me?" he started. "I asked you for the papers on the Jones's deal more than a week ago and told you I had to have them in three days. He tried to back out, and I almost lost that deal. I told you it was worth a hundred grand to me, and you promised to get them done. I bought a little more time, but if you can't make the deadline, I will be getting another attorney.

"We have been friends for twenty years, and you have been a terrific attorney for me. It looks to me as though this murder case you are working on has screwed up your timing and your practice. I need to know now whether you can get them done for me or not. I need them in hand by the day after tomorrow. You've been one of my best friends since fifth grade, I don't want to lose you. But if I don't have the papers by five tomorrow, I will have to find someone who will deliver."

There was nothing I could do but apologize abjectly and promise I would have them done and be there for him in the future. It was obvious I needed help badly. I didn't want a partner. I wanted a young lawyer who could learn quickly and work well with Stella. I walked out of the diner having finished my Reuben sandwich and ran into another client who stripped the rest of my skin off with a barrage of anger at my failure to get his work done. He had a long commercial lease that needed some work and my approval. A meeting was scheduled two days away in my office with his counterpart in the deal. I had known I was in trouble, but this was more serious than I had imagined and a terrible indictment. I had always prided myself that my clients came first, and here I was in violation of my most basic precept as an attorney. I was suddenly nauseous and so angry at myself that there seemed no solution. I was near the courthouse and headed for Judge Blevin's office.

I leveled with him and asked him if any young attorney had shown promise in his courtroom. He surprised me with an almost instant recommendation.

"You may not want to consider a woman," he said, "but Mary Steele is the best new attorney I have seen since you came to town. She's married with a child and a husband. He's a new architect. She finished Wayne Law School at the head of her class while working nights to help sup-port both herself and her husband as they finished their degrees. She was just in my office and told me she's looking for a job. She doesn't have trial experience to speak of, but I think she will be special in a year or two. She may be just what you need. By the way, don't cut yourself up too badly. This is a learning experience. I know you, and I know you will find a way to handle it."

"How do I find her?" I asked.

He gave me her number, and I reached her on the first try. I invited her to the same diner where Jesse had nailed me to the wall. She was personable. Her husband had just gotten an entry-level job with a firm. She told me she wanted a job as well.

We talked about the law and what she hoped to accomplish as an attorney. I immediately liked her and told her about my practice in Darien, a few miles from Flint where we were meeting. I told her I was under the gun on a number of matters I had neglected while working on Betty's case and needed someone right away.

"The thing is, I have a young child and child care has to be available close to where I work," she said.

"I don't think that will be a problem," I reassured her, thinking of the good childcare available in Darien. "And your hours can be flexible as long as the work gets done on time."

She asked what her salary would be and seemed pleased at the figure I offered. After a very short discussion, we agreed she would start tomorrow and meet in my office to go over the work that needed immediate attention. Stella had been holding clients off for way too long, and I knew she was going to be thrilled at Mary's appearance. No matter how strongly recommended, Mary was going to face multiple problems with clients whose cases I'd been letting slide.

The next morning, I met her at my office. Stella and I finished the real estate papers and called Jesse to tell him they were ready for pickup. I followed up the call and doubled down on my apology. I spent the rest of the day on the commercial lease for the upcoming meeting, and Stella worked with Mary on our office procedures and caught her up on the cases that needed immediate attention. We had a number of documents, including several wills, land contracts and minor collection cases for the bank that needed work.

At noon, I took her to lunch at the local restaurant and introduced her to everybody there. After lunch, we headed to the bank where she met Frank Matthews, the president and a good client. I had been handling the bank's business for a couple of years, and I was hopeful Frank wouldn't have a problem with Mary stepping in for a period of time. He was tentative because she lacked experience but said he liked her. So long as I was available by phone and provided oversight, he thought we could continue working together. I breathed a sigh of relief since the bank business was dependable money for the firm.

It was obvious she had a solid grounding in the law. We headed back to the office for the afternoon where Stella laid out the forms we use in the various business situations on the conference table. The two of them picked my brain on how I wanted to proceed, and we spent a productive, few hours.

I left them working hard and apparently well together. With Mary's warm personality, she made friends quickly. I had the feeling she would be welcomed in my small town, and that was a real plus. She and Stella had apparently hit it off instantly and they began to take charge of my neglected cases like old pros.

I was again absorbed by Betty's case the next day. When I called the day after next, Stella answered on the first ring with "Nichols and Steele, how may we help you?"

I laughed and asked if my name was still on the door. Stella laughed with me.

"How is Mary doing?"

She gave me a gushing report, a good sign for the future. Mary had taken hold without a problem, and aside from some questions she had regarding a couple of my cases, Stella thought everything was under control.

"I'm telling clients that Mary is a pro, a top-notch attorney capable of handling their matters when you aren't there."

"I agree," I said. "And let's change our door sign to Nichols, Steele and Associates."

I was relieved. I had to focus on Betty's defense and had little interest in handling the nuts and bolts of my normal practice. Mary came on the line, and I thanked her for saving my practice. "Don't worry boss," she said. "Stella and I have this." From that moment on, I knew I had two fighters in my corner. A huge relief.

CHAPTER 19

Deering's Dynamite

I **called Dr. Ben Deering** to get an update on his find-ings. He had a sobering assessment. Betty had indeed told me the truth – her injuries simultaneously helped prove the case and spun me into a funk. What had been done to her was beyond anything I could ever imagine. I had to shake it off. I headed to the jail to bring Betty up to speed on developments. She was putting a good face on things, although there was no way in the gray gloom of that jail cell to know for sure how she was really feeling. I got permission to meet in what they called the attorneys' room, which was comparatively better, although hardly comfortable. I had been there before but she filled the room with her presence, despite the shapeless orange jail scrubs.

She fixed her eyes on mine with a mute appeal, and I spent the next hour telling her about the case progress. When I told her that Dr. Deering's exam revealed layers of scar tissue and recommended surgical revision, tears filled her eyes.

"You'll never be able to look at me without remembering

that ugliness," she said.

"Trust me," I said. "You survived and if you could see your own beauty, your own character, you wouldn't think like that." It was as if my words had lifted her head physically, and she looked at me. "Do you really believe that?"

"With all my heart," I said.

"Do you believe there is any chance of winning at all?" she asked.

"Yes," I said, "if the jury believes you, but no guarantee. I can't tell you how much I want to win this."

"Bob, do you know how much I have missed you?" she said softly.

She came into my arms, as naturally as though no time had passed since high school. It had been more than ten years. My feelings for her were pulling me, but I stopped. It wasn't the possible long-term prison sentence hanging over her. It was the ethics and emotions problem. For good reason, there are ethics rules against having relations with clients, and for equally good reason there are taboos about any relationships that could interfere with professional judgment. Hope and belief can cloud things horribly. I remembered Rob's admonition to avoid starting a new relationship with Betty while trying to defend her. But I had to face the fact it had become increasingly difficult to keep my feelings at bay.

She was close to the breaking point. She leaned on my shoulder, and we sat together for almost an hour without talking. I alternated between despair at my own stupidity and hopelessness at my attraction to her.

CHAPTER 20

Preparing Betty

I headed for the jail the first thing the next morning. It was time to prepare her trial testimony. She greeted me warmly as always, but with a carefulness as if she sensed my concerns.

We sat apart on the bunk, and I started the briefing on what to expect.

I'd told her it was typical for a murder suspect not to testify. It opened a defendant up to a blistering attack. If she missed a beat or misstated a fact, it would become the prosecutor's flag to wave over the case, proving she was not truthful.

"The truth is what you have and all you have," I said. "You're up for testifying, right? No one else can describe what went on in that house before the day of the incident. I think, given your story, you need to lay a foundation for the expert medical and psychological testimony. Are you with me?"

"Robert, you know I am with you, no matter what."

That was exactly not what I wanted to hear. It was

exactly the problem caused by a love relationship with the client – she would do whatever I told her instead of analyzing what I was saying.

But we had crossed that bridge when I realized I was falling for her and didn't contain the damage. I took a deep breath and focused again on her prep.

"I'll question you first, and O'Bannon will go second. You must listen to me, answer my question simply and truthfully, unless I use the words, 'Tell the jury.'"

I was watching her, making my eyes hard, to help make my point. "Do you get this?"

She nodded.

"I don't want to scare you out of telling your story, but this is not a storytelling exercise; this is a jury trial. You get this?" I wanted to make it a lecture so it would stick like it was pinned to her brain.

"Simple. Truthful. I answer you unless you tell me to speak longer to the jury," she said.

She had got it even better than I thought. We were grooved, and I felt a flush of confidence.

I went on. "During my direct examination, I'll give you an opportunity to describe Sam's mistreatment to the jury. Remember, you are describing it to the jury, not to me. You'll mention the shotgun, the injuries inside and out, and call it what it was – rape. But we won't sound like we're sensationalizing. The jury can reach its own judgment on this without any prodding. As horrible as it is, if you or I sensationalize it, we'll lose the jury."

I was explaining a nuance that cannot be exactly explained, only hinted at, but she took it in and nodded.

"In his cross-examination, O'Bannon will attack you for your use of the term 'rape.' He'll goad you to say you killed him because he raped you. You cannot go there, because if you do the judge will instruct the jury that the law says a husband's rape is not a legal justification for self-defense. I've told you that already, right?"

She nodded. I had never had a client who followed me

so intensely. Maybe our wrong-headed relationship was actually doing something good for the case.

"You simply say, 'I was asked a question about what he did so I answered it.' And you look at him straight in the eye, but with no anger at him. He's not the target; Waterman is.

"O'Bannon will assume that the men on the jury will resent any implication that forcing sex on their wives could ever be considered rape. He'll point out the law in that regard, but I think the jury will hold it against him for making a legal point that seems unfair as hell."

Betty just nodded. Her lips were pinched together in concentration. Her hands were clenched, and I had a strange awareness of her strength.

"It's going to be difficult to discuss these intimate details in open court," I said. "It will take all your courage to do it.

"Once O'Bannon asks about 'rape,' he will have opened the door, and you have the right to give a complete answer that ends with 'and that is why I believed him when he said he would kill me and burn Beth alive.'"

She shuddered involuntarily, and I quickly apologized.

"Betty, you'll win the jury if you remain strong enough to answer, but soft enough to remain the victim, not the aggressor. You *were* the victim, and I hope you know that in your heart."

Then I threw the curve I needed to prepare her for.

"So if it really was so terrible, why did you stay?" I said it with an edge that caught her breath for an instant, and then she understood we were play acting with the most important question of the trial.

Her voice was steady and she looked me in the eye as if I were a total stranger.

"He allowed me no money, he swore he would hunt me down and kill both of us if I tried to leave. Beth was his child legally, you understand, and he would always have rights and a way to get her back and kill her, and he would always rape me as often as he liked."

The simplicity of her words was breathtaking.

It took several seconds to regain my composure, because in the short moments it took her to answer my accusation, I felt the force that O'Bannon would feel as she blew him away in front of the jury. O'Bannon was toast, if she answered that way at trial. I smiled just thinking about it.

I continued, but the stress of baking the story was now gone. We were at the frosting part.

"Betty, after O'Bannon is done, I'll get to stand up and do a short redirect examination. I'm going to throw you some soft pitches to hit out of the park."

Her eyes were bright with attention on me.

"I'm going to ask: When you picked up that shotgun that morning, were you going to kill Sam because he raped you?"

She hit it perfectly. "I had been raped so many times by my husband that at that point I was not even thinking of that."

"If you were not thinking about being raped, what then were you thinking about?"

"I was," and she sobbed, "only thinking of Beth being shoved into that furnace, screaming, terrified as she caught on fire."

A long sob broke from her throat.

I reached for her and enveloped her in my arms.

"I'm sorry, Betty, I am so sorry. I am so sorry," I said over again. Her head shook against my chest.

"I know. I know," she said. "You had to ask it."

"Betty, we will never speak of it again, but now you know what is going to happen, and why it has to happen."

I pushed her away gently, and said, "I will have two questions after that, and you have to try to concentrate and answer them."

Once again assuming a courtroom character, I said, "So Betty, when you picked up that shotgun and you had that vision of Beth, what happened next?"

It was the walk-off hit. "I suddenly heard a sound in my head like 'NOOOOOOO,' and suddenly there was an explosion and I looked down and he was horrible ...," and she broke down again.

The jury would already have seen the photos, courtesy of O'Bannon's blustery opening statement, so no explanation was necessary.

"The last question will be, 'Do you know what caused that shotgun to go off?'"

In character, she said, "No, I didn't aim or think about it or intend to shoot it." Her head shook slightly, as if subtly puzzling over what had happened.

"That's it," I said, and relaxed.

"But what if he accuses me of lying?" she asked.

"Do not be defensive. Did you run away?" She responded by shaking her head. "Did you hide the body or the gun?" She shook her head again. "Did you try to make up some alibi?" Head shake. "Were you horrified by what you saw on the bed?"

It was a question I liked to use, helping a defendant side with the jury's same reaction, instead of denying it.

She put her hands over her eyes and dropped her head so her hair hung down and sighed. "It was so shocking I will never get over seeing it."

I headed back to the office and did busy work with a feeling of lightness I had not felt in days. Trial preparation is not the last word. We still had a trial, and I knew now that Betty and I had established the crucial link every trial lawyer needs with the client. She was tuned in fully to the case, the language, the words, and the meaning between the words.

Stella, Mary and I cleaned up my desk.

CHAPTER 21

Researching Potential Jurors

On **November 1,** the list of potential jurors had been posted for the next ninety-day term of circuit court trials, which would begin in December. I picked up copies of the individual questionnaires each potential juror had filed at the circuit court clerk's office. There were seventy-five names, and we needed to know everything available about each of them.

I met with Jim at his office to discuss how to collect the information. Of course, we couldn't directly contact them since it would create an appearance of jury tampering. However, nothing prevented a comprehensive background check, including questioning their friends and examining the public record to make sure their answers were truthful.

There is always a fairly large number of people who want to be jurors in high-profile cases, not always for the best of reasons. Some have a personal agenda, usually coming from a strong bias for or against the defendant. We needed to find anyone who could approach the case with a clear bias, starting with the answers they gave on the court's questionnaire.

"This is a full-time job," Jim said, "and I will need help."

I told him not to worry about the cost and to retain whatever help he needed. It worried me though. I had long spent Tom's small retainer and was already depleting my nest egg. But we both knew our ability to gauge each juror was tremendously important, perhaps the most important key to success at trial. I left the meeting and headed over to talk to Rob, who could help us.

I told him we had started our juror investigation, and I needed his expertise as a psychologist in creating an ideal juror profile. I also wanted Rob's take on the kind of juror we must avoid. I was sure Jerry would emphasize Betty's college record, her intelligence, and, subliminally, her appearance. He would assume, and I had to agree, that non-college educated women could resent her looks and her brains. If a female juror believed Betty was a little uppity, she might accept the proposition that Betty deserved whatever she got.

"At the same time," I added, "there are certain to be men in the jury pool who sympathize with Sam, the all-American, NRA teacher, who expected and demanded that Betty fulfill her wifely duties. He was a good high school football player, and so far as I know, his police record is clean. The fact that rape by a husband is not a crime in Michigan will give these men cover to overlook the worst parts of Sam's actions."

I've always felt that educated women make the best jurors in almost every type of case – they are more willing to listen to all the testimony before jumping to conclusions, and their level of understanding tends to be superior. In Betty's case we needed to get them past the initial shock and graphic images of the killing in order to absorb the rest of the testimony.

I gave Rob copies of the questionnaires and we scheduled a meeting for a week later. He promised his evaluation and suggestions based on the forms with the understanding that we would be meeting in depth later when Jim's report was available.

CHAPTER 22

Jury Voir Dire

It **would take Jim three weeks** to put together the jurors' evaluation report. Meanwhile, I worked at the office, attempting to save my law practice. One client had already given up in disgust, and there was quite a list of local clients needing my personal attention. And as nice and competent as Mary was, most clients wanted to meet with me face-to-face to tackle the complexities of their cases. If we lost any more accounts, I would need to start really worrying about the mounting costs of Betty's case.

Stella and Mary had managed to make almost everyone else feel tended to. Sitting with several of the town's residents and sharing stories from Betty's case for a few hours had been salutary. My stories spread throughout the town, and Darien's feelings began to shift in Betty's favor. I also spent a lot of time with Betty using repetition and discussion of our trial strategy. Over time, she was able to answer almost any question without hesitation or the appearance of dissembling.

I met with Rob and Jim at Rob's office and we sat down

to look at the jury pool. Rob had a big chalkboard, where a value was assigned to each juror on the list. A number one was someone we felt confident would listen to the entire case and come to the trial without an assumption of guilt. A number two would be a juror without obvious flaws but a background that might support a guilty verdict. Number three would be individuals we did not want on the jury for a number of reasons, and number fours would be those subject to motions to challenge for cause. We all understood that Betty had the final say on jurors called since her intuition would be of greater importance than the background materials we had accumulated. If she liked someone or believed a potential juror didn't like her, we would act accordingly.

Both the prosecution and defense are given twelve peremptory challenges that allow removal of any juror without explanation. There would also be challenges to remove jurors with explanation, making me worry the jury pool of seventy-five might not be large enough. If that happened, new names would be added without much time to check them out. I would have to rely on a personal examination of each juror whose name was picked to sit on the jury. Fortunately, Judge Blevin preferred to allow the attorneys to handle the exam.

I had defined the areas of concern and prepared a list of questions for each juror as he or she was picked at random by the clerk. After the routine questions about whether the juror knew someone involved in the trial or had a relationship with the police or prosecutor's office, I intended to ask about the potential juror's feelings about abuse and sexual assault, including marital assault. I had spent a number of hours with Betty since she would be the final arbiter if we disagreed on a juror. I printed up our ideas and handed them to Rob and Jim for their comments. I hoped my list handled every issue and wanted their informed comments as to potential changes in the list.

First, I would ask whether the juror or the juror's family

or friends had been the victim of a crime and, if so, had the courts been fair to them or given appropriate treatment to the criminal? I would ask how the juror felt about the jury system. Did he or she believe in the jury system and whether he or she was pleased to be chosen a juror in a criminal case?

I would then go into rape as sexual assault and ask whether the juror believed a husband should be able to rape his wife. For those who thought a husband should be able to legally rape his wife, I would ask what level of force would change his or her mind.

Then, on the question of self-defense, I would ask whether the juror believed that you should be able to use lethal force to defend a member of your family from certain death.

On temporary insanity, I would ask if the juror believed a defendant should be allowed to use the defense of temporary insanity to excuse a homicide. Then I would ask about whether the juror had heard of irresistible impulse and whether he or she understands it.

Finally, I would ask if the juror will be able to vote not guilty if the testimony supported the elements of that defense as explained by the judge.

We had an extended discussion at this point. Rob agreed with my conclusions on the best juror for us and was worried that the men on the panel included a large number of hunters and sportsmen who loved high school sports and shooting. Michigan was one of the leading states for deer hunting. These were Sam's visible attributes as a high school football star and crack shot. A lot of guys would transpose them into thinking he was a regular guy doing regular things they personally enjoyed. It wouldn't be too much of a leap to sympathize with Sam over his complaining wife.

The only redeeming feature would be education and that was just a start on what we needed to know. I left them matching Jim's findings and the questionnaires.

They intended to work together for as many meetings as were required to have recommendations for each juror. We needed a lot of luck with the composition of the jury, but they had impressed me with their perception and obvious enjoyment of each other as professionals. We were ready to try the case with a little more polishing.

It was another few weeks before they brought their conclusions to me, and the results were poor on almost every level. There were only seventeen women and five men on the panel who could be rated as number ones and almost thirty potential jurors flirting with or meeting the criteria for number threes. Another ten would be subject to reasonable success with challenges for cause and the balance were twos – not particularly good prospects for the defense.

Meantime the trial date crept closer than I liked. I still had monumental nervousness, and then, finally, the date arrived.

Betty, Rob, Jim and I crowded together at the counsel table as the members of the jury pool walked into the courtroom. There seemed to be an air of not just anticipation but enjoyment in the air. Most people knew each other and smiled and exchanged greetings. Jerry and John Stevens, his state police chief investigator, sat at another table a nice distance away before the judge's seat. The clerk sat on the judge's left between him and the jury box. She had the container on her table there, ready to draw the names of the first set of potential jurors. The process called for pulling twelve names and placing the named potential jurors in their jury box seats, numbered one through twelve. We would address them by their number, not their names.

Judge Blevin entered and was introduced by the bailiff with a ceremony that has persisted for the entire life of courts in America.

"Hear ye, hear ye, hear ye, the Seventh Judicial Circuit Court is now in session, the Honorable Judge Blevin is presiding."

CHAPTER 23

Judge Blevin Welcomes the Jurors

Judge Blevin welcomed the seventy-five jurors and gave them instructions. Jerry and I had heard his rote speech many times but understood how important it was for the judge to lay down the rules of the trial. I assumed most of the jurors had at least a minimal understanding of what was expected, but Judge Blevin thoroughly detailed the do's and don'ts.

He emphasized the jury's preeminent position as the determiner of the facts. He made it clear they were to only consider testimony from the stand and disregard statements of facts by counsel.

"The defendant has pled not guilty to this charge of first-degree murder. The charge is not evidence and you must not think it is evidence of her guilt," he told the jury, his voice strong but not pompous. "This case is based solely on the evidence presented within the courtroom. You must take the law as the judge rules, but as jurors, you are the ones who will decide this case. When the time comes to decide the case, you are allowed to consider only the evidence that was admitted in the case. It is your job to decide what the facts of this case are. Which witnesses you believed and how important their testimony is. In deciding which testimony you believe, you should rely on your common sense and everyday experience. Finally, the prosecutor must prove each element of the crime beyond a reasonable doubt."

He left a parting note before the jury selection began.

"During this trial, the defendant is not required to take the stand to prove her innocence. She is not required to do anything."

CHAPTER 24

Jury Selection.

The jurors were assigned individual numbers. Juror number one (we use the juror number in this process, not a person's name) was a professional man whom we had rated on the high end of number two.

The rest of the jurors comprised a mixed bag – we had assigned five with the top rating of a one, with the rest getting a two or three. The prosecutor had the first chance at voir dire – examining the juror – and began by establishing that number one had no friends in the police force or was connected with the prosecution or defense in any way. He was an accountant, married with two young children. His wife had read about the case and asked him whether he would be on that jury. They had not discussed it at any length, although both knew the bare bone details of the shooting. Jerry established he would have no difficulty in finding a woman guilty if the evidence supported that verdict.

"I turn the exam over to you, Mr. Nichols," he said.

I asked number one if he had had prior crimes against

his family – "No" – and his fundamental feelings about the jury system. Next, I talked about rape as sexual assault, forcing or coercing an individual to engage in any nonconsensual sexual contact or sexual penetration. I told him in Michigan a husband can legally rape his wife.

"Do you believe a husband should be able to rape his wife?" I asked.

"No," he said, shaking his head. "I definitely do not."

I then gave him the definition of self-defense as the act of defending oneself or one's family, through the use of force.

"Do you believe that you should be able to use lethal force to defend a member of your family from certain death?"

"Yes," he said.

I told him that the defendant and our expert Dr. Rob Willoby would testify to a defense of temporary insanity by reason of irresistible impulse.

"Do you believe a defendant should be allowed to use the defense of temporary insanity to excuse a homicide?" I asked.

He hesitated.

"That's a good question. I'd have to think about it," he said. "Maybe I would, if the facts were clear and unambiguous."

"Have you ever heard of the defense of irresistible impulse as one form of temporary insanity?" I asked.

"No, not really," he said. "I'm not sure what it means."

"If the judge tells you that irresistible impulse is a possible defense in this case, would you be able to vote not guilty if the testimony supports the elements of that defense as explained by the judge?" I asked.

"Yes," he said.

The prosecutor began his questioning of juror number two, and there were no surprises.

But when I asked my series of questions, it turned out that this man was far less sure of his responses. He wouldn't give me a direct "yes" or "no." I saw red flags.

Jerry and I asked the first twelve jurors the same questions we had asked the first juror. When we finished with the last juror, Judge Blevin asked if there were any challenges for cause. Jerry immediately challenged number seven for her friendly relationship with a police officer and was sustained. He was grandstanding for the jury, appearing to be concerned about justice. Yet he knew that I, too, would have challenged for cause if he didn't. I passed on any challenges for cause.

Jerry then challenged juror number one, the accountant who said he'd consider all elements of the defense. We challenged number eight. Betty said in conference that she sensed her antagonism, and both Jim and Rob agreed this woman would be bad news. Accordingly, I exercised my first peremptory challenge and dismissed her from the jury.

It was Jerry's turn again, and he challenged number eleven. This was a gift to us since we didn't like this juror, either.

The clerk pulled the names of three more jurors to replace the challenges and we began the questioning all over again. We now had nine jurors, who would support self-defense of a member of the family if the circumstances were sufficient to justify use of lethal force. There was the expected reluctance to endorse irresistible impulse, but everyone indicated a willingness to listen to the judge about its definition and how to apply it.

After questioning the three new jurors, I felt willing to go with them, worried that the jurors waiting in the panel pool might be even worse. I asked Rob, Jim and Betty how they felt about the jury already seated. It was relatively vanilla at this point with no single threat that set off alarm bells. I did intend to challenge juror number two. Those red flags bothered me.

Surprisingly, we shared the feeling that we were close to having a jury as good as we had hoped for. Jerry passed on using another peremptory challenge, and I challenged juror two. Sure enough, the replacement was an atrocious man with a three rating. Jerry again passed, and I challenged the replacement for juror two. This time the replacement was a retired teacher, a mother with grown children and a number one rating.

When Jerry passed again, we had a jury that was better at every level than we had hoped for. We were close to 4:30 in the afternoon and Judge Blevin opted to close for the day. We ended the day with a conference at the counsel table. I told Jim, Rob and Betty that I didn't expect the prosecutor would take long with his opening statement in the morning.

"I'm pretty sure he feels like he's got a slam dunk and will pound away at Betty's physical ability to leave the home with Beth as the antidote to self-defense. And he considers irresistible impulse a desperation ploy not worthy of his concern. At least that's what he told me a few days ago."

Our whole team agreed the jury was better for us than we had any right to expect, the first really positive feeling we had all shared. Not a single number three had made it on the jury, and that was astonishing, given the makeup of the overall jury panel available.

Betty was clearly relieved and gave us the first smile we had seen in a long time before she was escorted back to her cell.

CHAPTER 25

Elsa Attacks

I was leaving the courtroom with Jim and Rob when I heard some kind of melee behind me in the hallway. As I turned to see what the disturbance was, I felt a huge blow in my back and felt myself falling with a sharp pain behind my shoulder. There was more loud noise – the blast of a gun – as I felt the heavy weight of someone falling on me.

"I'll kill you!" rang out a woman's voice.

That was the last thing I remembered before I woke up in a hospital bed with Stella and Rob huddled beside me with welcoming smiles.

"What happened?" I asked.

"I'm sure glad you're back," Rob said. "It's been a long time. It was Sam's girlfriend, Elsa. She shot you and Jim. Jim recognized her as she charged across the hallway and tried to stop her. She got away from him, at least long enough to point the gun and shoot you in the back before he could grab the gun away from her. Jim took her second shot in his chest and somehow tore the gun from her before falling over you.

"Ben was there, luckily, and used a compress to stop Jim's bleeding, all the while shouting at the top of his lungs for an ambulance," Rob added

Rob told me Elsa's first bullet had gone in through my

back, just off center, and, fortunately for me, missed my major organs and arteries.

"Jim's wound is infinitely more serious," Rob said. "He was transported to the hospital in minutes and went into surgery immediately. The bullet went through his left lung and lodged right near a major artery. It caused a double puncture in the lung and severe tissue damage. The doctor said that Ben's quick response gave him a fighting chance."

"Is he going to be okay? Am I going to be okay?" I asked, worried.

Their smiles told me I was going to be fine.

"We've been waiting for you to wake up from the drugs, which made you sleep," Rob said. "You needed them to fight a possible infection. The docs don't think you'll have any long-term effects, but Jim is still in intensive care after an eight-hour surgery. They had to do a hugely risky surgical maneuver to get the bullet out from near his artery. It's still touch and go. He has a fifty-fifty chance of surviving this."

Rob told me again that Jim saved my life, actually tackling Elsa just as her gun was poised to finish me off. He had taken the second shot meant for me.

"His wife, Olivia, is waiting outside the ICU. She's pretty much a wreck."

I was overwhelmed with grief and guilt. Still in a fog of painkillers, I had a hell of a time absorbing all the details, but clearly understood Jim was a hero. I spent long hours thinking about it. Maybe Elsa's real goal was to attack Betty, but she couldn't get near enough because of the deputies escorting her to jail. Since she couldn't kill Betty, she decided she'd go for me. She apparently waited for me to walk out of the courtroom. When I opened the door, she charged toward me with such force, knocking someone down in the process. No one could stop her. Jim immediately recognized her and handled the emergency like a pro. I owed him.

CHAPTER 26

The Plight of Jim Drew

We all were severely depressed by Jim's condition and waiting on pins and needles for word on his prognosis.

As for the trial, it was immediately delayed while Judge Blevin awaited news of my condition and Jim's. Rob said Betty had been devastated by the attack, and he went to the jail, trying to reassure her. I knew it would be a long time before we could be ready to continue the trial, and Jim's condition would be the determining factor. I made it clear that I was not going to be ready until Jim was ready, assuming he survived.

I'd been in the hospital for a couple of days, when Ben and another doctor came in and cleared the room for an exam. Ben told me that everything looked good and that I should be good to go in a week or so. He introduced Dr. Reynolds, Jim's supervising surgeon, who shared what he had faced when Jim hit the operating room. "They had to stop the internal and external bleeding while evaluating the initial scope of the wound. As you know, the bullet penetrated his left lung, front and back, and lodged in close proximity to one of the main arteries servicing Jim's heart. His lung was collapsed with his breathing limited. In medical terms, Jim had suffered a traumatic pneumothorax from direct trauma to the chest from a gunshot with associated major internal bleeding, tissue trauma and the additional danger of the bullet lodged in such a difficult position."

Dr. Reynolds described the surgery, including how they had stopped the bleeding, removed the bullet with surgical precision, and inserted a tube for air drainage and removal of excess blood and fluid buildup to help inflate the lung.

"We suctioned out blood cells and other fluids in the pleural space. The tube will be left in place for several more days until Jim's chest can fully expand," Reynolds said.

"What's the prognosis for Jim?" I asked.

"Better than fifty-fifty, assuming no infection or intervening trouble from adverse reactions to the medicines used in his treatment. It usually takes six to eight weeks to fully recover from a punctured lung and possibly more if we get a major complication of shock that comes with infection. There's also a risk of severe inflammation or the development of excess fluid in the damaged lung, which could lead to cardiac arrest."

I asked for a phone to call Judge Blevin and Jerry. It was close to noon, and I got through quickly. I gave him the news that Jim's recovery might take a while.

"I'll recess the trial for a month," Blevin said. "I hope we'll have enough good news on Jim to allow us to set a firm date down the road."

I went back to sleep. A few days later, I was healthy enough to join Olivia in her solitary vigil at the ICU while Jim fought for his life. Otherwise, we sat there as if our presence could lend healing. One evening, Jim took a turn for the worse. A nurse soberly gave us the news.

"We've given Jim some powerful drugs to fight the infection, and we've put him in the coma to let his body use all its resources to heal, but it's slow going."

Olivia had managed to keep his condition safe from their four-year-old son, Jim Jr.

I pinned every hope I had on Jim's recovery, almost as a personal measure of belief in the world. When Olivia reminisced about his earlier battles with injury and line-of-duty disability, I just took it as an omen of things to come. I grew into his family as if I were blood. His recovery became the linchpin for our trial strategy.

It turned out that Ben was on the mark. I started to feel normal in about two weeks and was rested and ready. Jim, although he was on the mend, would not be ready for at least six more weeks. The judge accommodated me and pushed the trial commencement date another two months down the road.

I spent most of the time during those intervening weeks alternating between Jim and Olivia in his hospital room and Betty in the county jail. Mary helped me reestablish ties with clients. There was a steady stream through the office, wanting to make sure I was all right and wanting to bathe in some of the reflected light of the highest profile lawyer in Darien. Since I was the only lawyer in Darien, it was easy to maintain that profile.

Getting shot had its rewards. The newspaper reports of my shooting had been a sensation, and the town buzzed with speculation about Betty's case. Elsa, as Sam Waterman's mistress, had splashed mud on that side of the ledger. Betty had an inside track or at least it felt that way.

Betty and I talked more deeply about our mutual feelings and the years we'd lost apart since high school.

The waiting was agony for her. Depression over her separation from Beth was a constant battle, but we arranged weekly visits to dull the pain and longing.

The future was the only taboo topic. She was a defendant facing possible life imprisonment. Michigan didn't have a death penalty, but it had a living death penalty.

The trial started to keep me awake again. I was nagged

by the phantom missing fact – evidence to corroborate her belief that Sam would kill her and Beth that morning. The most important element in our defense was still only that belief. A smoking gun of innocence is an oxymoron. You can't prove a negative that she had no intent to kill. But that's what gnawed at me for a response.

The next day, the trial commenced and the jury came into the courtroom smiling at me, many nodding a welcome. They all seemed to have read about Elsa's attack in the local paper. It was not part of the trial and, therefore, permissible reading under the court's instructions. Elsa's romantic connection to Sam, of course, came out, unassailable proof he was a lousy husband at the very least.

Jim had managed to point a reporter to the police reports he had found disclosing Elsa's prior charges – she became known as the schizophrenic other woman of Sam's. Jim was now considered a hero for disarming Elsa and taking a shot for me and saving my life.

Judge Blevin welcomed me back with a short speech to the jury.

"A lot has happened in the last three months. I want to make sure all of you understand sympathy for the defense attorney, Bob Nichols, and Jim Drew, his investigator, is appropriate but should not influence your findings of fact.

"I'd like to remind you of my remarks when you appeared for jury selection. The only evidence you can rely upon is what you hear in this courtroom from the stand. Now I would like to invite Prosecutor Jerry O'Bannon to make his opening statement before the jury in support of the charge of first-degree murder."

Judge Blevin briefly described the purpose of opening statements – an outline of the facts, not argument – partly for the jury's context, but mostly to remind us lawyers to keep away from the grandiose pronouncements and opinions dramatized in television trials.

CHAPTER 27

The Trial Begins: Prosecution's Opening Statement

Before **Jerry could start,** I made a motion that all listed witnesses be removed from the courtroom until called, excluding the prosecution's investigator, John Nelson, and my own investigator, James Drew.

Judge Blevin agreed and ordered all witnesses to immediately leave the courtroom and to remain out of listening distance.

This ensured witnesses for the prosecution could not hear and use testimony by other witnesses to buttress their own. After they had filed out, O'Bannon took his position at the podium facing the jury with an air of a racehorse ready to bolt. It was out of place with the placid atmosphere set by Judge Blevin, and two of the jurors' eyebrows arched with something like humor. Another fancy lawyer.

"Ladies and gentlemen of the jury," he began with the voice of an orator, "my name is Jerry O'Bannon. I am the prosecutor for this county and will be presenting the people's overwhelming testimony and evidence in this case.

"Betty Waterman, the defendant sitting there at the counsel table, is charged with the brutal, first-degree murder of her husband, Sam Waterman, in their home on the morning of October fourth last year. We will prove beyond a reasonable doubt that she killed him with a single shotgun blast while he laid there. Sleeping peacefully in bed. She has admitted that she and their three-year-old daughter, Beth, were the only others in the home, and she has confessed to firing the shot that killed her husband."

His first mistake. She'd admitted to holding the gun, not to firing it.

"Ladies and gentlemen, she has also admitted that he was asleep at the time she killed him, and was unarmed when he died. We will introduce pictures of the terrible and fatal wound he suffered from her shotgun blast.

"I assume you will hear smoke and mirrors and razzle-dazzle from the defense attorney in a desperate attempt to convince you that, somehow, the killing was justified as an act of self-defense."

There was my opening and I took it. "Your Honor," I said, long enough to make O'Bannon pause as I rose, "I object to the characterization. As your honor said, opening statements are for the presentation of facts and not argument or opinion." I sat down again.

"Sustained," Blevin said and lightly cracked the dais with his palm. Nothing more but that, and it was enough.

O'Bannon cleared his throat and touched the knot of his tie, as if it were too tight. I could read the signs. He was downsizing his bombast into facts to avoid another objection, which he knew would come if he left me another opening. He'd started without thinking, and now he had to think fast.

"As I was saying," he tried to alibi the judge's ruling, "Mr. Nichols will present facts of alleged prior abuse by the victim to rationalize his client's act of murder."

I pursed my lips in disapproval, no more than that, my sign to show the jury O'Bannon was not to be believed. Too much reaction was worse than no reaction at all.

He went on, "Prior abuse is irrelevant. Michigan law, as the judge will tell you, says the defendant must prove she was in fear of imminent attack or harm from her husband. Imminent means immediate, as in right now. It doesn't mean what happened last night or last week, or what might happen in the future." He slowed to let that point resonate.

"The facts will show there was no imminent threat. Mr. Waterman was asleep. Defenseless. He was sleeping when she shot him. Nothing prevented her from walking out of the house and taking her daughter that morning. The notion that he had told her he intended to kill her and their child in the morning is ..." He had to pause to edit whatever sarcastic word he'd started to utter, and the jury knew it as if it had already been uttered in violation of the judge's ruling. He finished lamely. "Well, the facts won't show that, ladies and gentlemen.

"There was no threat of imminent harm from him at the moment he was killed. He was not leaping at her from the bed with a weapon of any kind. He was not speaking to her so as to threaten her with attack. He was just lying there sleeping as she killed him with a shotgun blast. Think about that. She took the choice to kill him rather than simply getting into her car and going to the police.

"If that defense seems absurd, think about the other

defense he plans to try to use as justification. He will claim the defendant was temporarily insane, under the control of irresistible impulse. The defendant will attempt to use the brazen, unproved story of irresistible impulse as a defense for the brutal murder of her husband. Does she think you are so dull and foolish as to fall for such a ridiculous story? How can a defense attorney remain credible when he attempts such chicanery?"

This time all I had to do was stand. Blevin was ready, without me saying a word. "Mr. O'Bannon," Judge Blevin said as a parent would, "I have already ruled once, and I do not want to rule again. You know what an opening statement is and what it is not."

The judge waved the back of his hand for O'Bannon to continue without even looking at him. The two jurors who had arched their eyebrows previously were now joined by four others. They'd enjoyed the spanking.

O'Bannon's face showed a deep flush, either anger or embarrassment, maybe both. He had made four mistakes – the judge had ruled against him twice, he'd misstated a key fact about a nonexistent admission, and he'd established me by name – Mr. Nichols.

It was a personal belief you never used the opposing attorney's name. It created a personality for him. I would call him "the prosecutor."

He gamely went on. There was a thin line of sweat forming along his sideburns. "Let me state what the facts will show. The defendant will complain to you that her husband actually raped her, perhaps even on a number of occasions. Those facts are irrelevant, inasmuch as Michigan does not recognize sexual assault by a husband as a criminal act. Whether you like it or not, Sam Waterman was entitled under the law to expect, in fact, to demand, that the defendant perform her wifely duties with him, including sexual consort."

It was too early to make that argument. Maybe if he'd showed the bloody photos first and set the scene for that statement, he could have made it. But coming right out of the starting gate telling a jury with seven women – six of them married – that their husbands could do whatever they wanted, "whether you like it or not," was strong stuff. From the looks on all seven faces, O'Bannon had hit a foul ball.

O'Bannon suddenly sensed he was headed downhill, but instead of creating some alibi like, "Sorry for that, but that's the law," he blustered on. Being a public official means never having to say you're sorry.

"Mr. Waterman had a right to require her services in bed and a right to demand that she perform those services. Her complaints that he demanded and occasionally forced her to perform sex with him ring hollow under the law and are irrelevant.

"Mr. Nichols may introduce evidence regarding Sam Waterman's conduct as a husband, including an alleged affair with another woman."

In fact, the story of his adultery made the headlines of the local paper and the lead story on the nightly news. Calling it 'alleged' was wishful thinking, and it registered as cheating on the faces of the entire jury.

"You must understand that this is immaterial under Michigan law. Other states have changed but not Michigan. We do not have the death penalty for murder, much less for out-of-wedlock affairs. In fact, there is no law of any kind that permits a private citizen to take the life of another unless there is justification defined as self-defense or temporary insanity."

He'd gotten to his best point, but it was too late. They were judging, not listening to him, and for the most part, except for two of the men I was watching from the corner of my eye, they weren't impressed.

"Judge Blevin will explain the law. It's your duty to follow that law. It's simple and straightforward: The defendant is required to be in fear of imminent attack or harm to herself or a member of her family in order to use self-defense. The key word is 'imminent.' Her story that he was going to kill her and Beth the next morning is asinine on its face."

I would have stood, but Judge Blevin beat me to it by clearing his throat with force, and several of the jury had to stifle laughs. O'Bannon had been reduced to the predictable role of one who just didn't get it.

He had to apologize, and he did it almost under his breath and then went on.

"The evidence will show it's not logical that someone would inform his proposed victim the night before that he intended to commit murder and then calmly go to sleep in the marital bed without restraining the victim in some manner to prevent escape?

"This claim of irresistible impulse fails the logic test and is a claim without facts to back it up."

He had finally got on track and would have sounded good if he'd done it right.

"The charge in this case is murder in the first degree. In order to find her guilty of first-degree murder, you will need to find premeditation. That won't be difficult in this case. Betty Waterman walked into the bedroom, reached under the bed for the shotgun, and shot her husband without compunction in a heartless way."

I made a note with an exclamation mark. Their shotgun – the one he raped her with.

O'Bannon's finish was coming, and I braced to make another objection. The oaf just could not contain himself.

"Ladies and gentlemen, the case will come down to this. Defendant Betty Waterman killed her husband with no legal justification. It was a horrible and depraved act. We will ask you, the jury, to perform your duty and find her guilty of first-degree murder."

I had been watching the jury through it all, and I had liked every reaction I'd seen.

Judge Blevin addressed me and asked if I was ready to present my opening statement.

"I'll reserve my opening statement until such time the

prosecutor rests and we commence the defense testimony."

I'd battled in my mind over the timing of my opening. It was routine to do one right after the prosecution's, to blunt what the jury had just learned. In this case, I knew to a certainty, I did not want to diminish what the judge had done, or what O'Bannon had done to himself.

Judge Blevin turned to O'Bannon and said, "The prosecution may proceed."

CHAPTER 28

Witnesses Testify for the Prosecution

Jerry called **Vince Brasso and John Stevens,** the state policemen involved. He established the date, location and admissions of the defendant. The police photos were admitted, including the bloody mess on the bed and the major bruises and black eye of the defendant.

On cross-examination, I established Betty had fully cooperated with the police, had surrendered peacefully and had been totally up front with the officers.

"Officer, could you tell me what you found in the furnace in the Waterman home?"

"We found the presence of the partial remains of a small cat in the furnace residue," Sergeant Stevens answered.

"And has the weapon used to kill Sam Waterman been in your continuous custody since found beside the bed in the defendant's home on the day of the shooting?"

"Yes sir," Sergeant Stevens confirmed. "I was present at the defense's examination of the gun and never out of sight of the gun during that examination."

Jerry then rested the prosecution and his reliance on a slam dunk was never more obvious.

It was the slightest, lightest murder case that had ever been presented. I wondered whether it was ego or strategy. My University of Hometown degree told me he had miscalculated. The community had got the sense – from the shootings, from Sam Waterman's reputation, from Betty's injuries – that the case was more complex than a single shot from a gun.

I looked at the jury. They were still hearing the faint echo of the kitten in the furnace and the threat to Betty's child.

Judge Blevin turned to me, and simply said, "Counsel."

"Ready, Your Honor," I said, and rose.

CHAPTER 29

Defense's Opening Statement

"Ladies and gentlemen of the jury, my name is Robert Nichols, and I represent the defendant, Betty Waterman.

"You have heard the prosecutor describe her as a murderer who took the life of her husband, Sam, without provocation. The officers described the nature of the wounds and described the injuries. We have seen photos of the deceased and a description of the police investigation. We have been told that Betty cooperated fully from the moment the shooting occurred and has never denied that she held the gun when it discharged. All in all, the prosecution has proved something that was a tragic accident.

"A shotgun in my client's hands went off, killing her husband." I turned the page of my notes. "It was not premeditated murder.

"I have to point out one glaring misstatement of fact by the prosecutor." This was the way to argue, without arguing. "He told you in his opening statement that Betty said she cocked the gun, and she pulled the trigger. Now you know that isn't true, don't you?" And I actually looked at the face of each juror, going to the next, because I wanted this fact to be imprinted with their participation.

"You know the MSP investigation report said, 'She admitted she was holding the shotgun and heard an explosion.' Now isn't that exactly what it says?" I asked.

I picked up the document, and turned to Judge Blevin. "Your Honor, may I approach the jury?" Some judges had an allergic reaction if any lawyer made so much as a single step toward the jury box. My request for permission was a bit of etiquette to show I respected his authority. I knew from experience what he'd say.

"You may approach for purposes of displaying evidence," he said easily.

I held up the document. "Look at page three, in the last full paragraph, please." I handed it to juror #1, then waited as he flipped to the paragraph and read it.

The document was passed to each juror. When the last one had finished and handed it back, I continued.

"Is the prosecutor right when he says Betty admitted she pulled the trigger?" And they all shook their heads no. That was the imprint.

"It *is* a fact that she had her eyes closed and she heard an explosion, isn't it?" Several of them nodded yes. "It is also a fact that Betty did not say she cocked that shotgun, and it is also a fact she did not release the safety on that shotgun, isn't it? The prosecutor was not correct, was he?"

Again, most of them shook their heads in agreement. The man on the end even caught on. He gave me his first positive reaction of the trial.

"There's no evidence about who or what caused that gun to fire." And now I was going to go out on a bit of a limb, and I hurried to get it in. "There's no dispute that she stood there with her eyes closed. Mr. Waterman was in bed, perhaps asleep, but was he really asleep? Did that man suddenly reach out and grab that gun, and pull his wife's finger onto the trigger and cause it to fire?"

I hurried, expecting an objection to speculation, but O'Bannon had been uncertain since I phrased the argument as a question.

I continued, and went on the attack. "The law, according to the prosecutor's opening statement, seems to be that husbands should get a free pass to sexually assault their wives any time they want and without any punishment and certainly without any concern for the woman. I am sure you, the jury," and I didn't say "you women," but they heard it just as I intended, "are surprised and perhaps shocked by this law in Michigan. You may also have noted the prosecutor said the husband could expect and, in fact, could demand something he described as 'wifely duties.'"

Sometimes a pause says more than words.

I adjusted my notes. "In his opening statement the prosecutor said Sam Waterman was entitled under the law to expect, in fact to demand, that the defendant perform her wifely duties with him. But as you know, the Michigan State Police officers did not say that. The prosecutor says it because he clearly believes the law is appropriate, not because it's literally true.

"It may be the opinion of the prosecutor, but I doubt if any of us believes it is fair to the women of Michigan or a good way to run our fair state or a nation.

"One of the fact witnesses you're going to hear is Betty's medical doctor, and one of the expert witnesses you're going to hear is the psychologist who evaluated her. They are going to talk about the scars, the mental damage done by a husband who raped and brutalized his wife. These witnesses are going to explain how a mind that is damaged by serial abuse – and I repeat, *serial abuse* – may lose control.

"Rape does exist in a marriage. Michigan law simply makes an exception allowing a husband to rape his wife without facing *a criminal charge*. This does not change the nature of violent rape or the scars it causes. It just lets the man off the hook, legally speaking. But the prosecutor's statement supporting rape immunity is incomplete.

"Rape – serial, long-time violence – creates mental and physical scars and that is what the evidence will show in this case. The mental scars are the kind that alter the mind, and that is what the facts show happened to Betty Waterman. Her body and mind were damaged, changed. She was changed."

I stopped for a moment, then stepped a little closer to the jury rail. I was going to make O'Bannon pay the price for not preparing. He'd committed the cardinal sin of failing to address my strongest evidence. Now, I would get a double advantage of introducing something the jury hadn't heard, and I'd highlight the telltale silence by the prosecutor.

"The facts in this case tell the tale of a woman who had been so controlled that she'd lost her ability to think clearly. She'd lost her ability to run. She'd lost her ability even to think. Why do you think a woman with Betty's intelligence would lose all that?"

Pause, to let the jury start making its own way toward my conclusion.

Then I said it. "He didn't mention the examination of the shotgun, did he?" I looked pointedly at O'Bannon, who looked quickly away.

"He didn't mention why Waterman burned the kitten to cinders, did he?" O'Bannon was pretending to make notes, and I fixed my stare on him and held it there until he looked up to see why nothing was happening. When our eyes locked, he winced perceptibly, and the jury saw it.

"You recall the shotgun testimony by the MSP officer? You recall the rape testimony? Well, we had that shotgun examined, and there was evidence of vaginal fluid up the barrel."

One of the women jurors spontaneously shouted, "No!"

"You recall the testimony about the incinerated kitten?

That was what Waterman promised to do to little Beth, if Betty didn't perform wifely services. The evidence in this case will show exactly why Betty couldn't run. Waterman would track her down and take his child, Beth. And the evidence will show exactly why Betty was too damaged to think anymore. Because she had been tortured, *raped* with a shotgun."

I stepped ever so slightly around the edge of the podium. "What the evidence will show is that Sam Waterman reaped what he sowed. He damaged the mind and emotions of his wife so that she was seized by an irresistible impulse. We'll never know if Waterman grabbed that shotgun and made it fire, or whether the uncontrolled voice in Betty's head took control and caused the gun to fire.

"But what we will see in this trial is that she never intended to fire that gun. That is a fact." I moved back to my notes.

"The prosecutor believes Waterman's immunity from prosecution can take the place of facts, and that he can convince you folks there is no justifiable homicide in Michigan. He argues Betty Waterman acted intentionally, with premeditation, to kill her husband. He told you he can prove every element of that offense.

"You may wonder why Betty didn't plead guilty and beg for his mercy? Because Betty's loss of control came in defense of her three-year-old daughter, Beth. She was holding the gun that shot Sam. But she had no more premeditation than you or I. She stood there in imminent fear for the life of Beth. The evidence will confirm that Sam was a psychopathic individual who committed atrocities upon Betty, and either Waterman did something to cause that gun to go off or divine intervention caused it.

"Judge Blevin told you the defendant does not have to testify. But Betty *is* going to testify. She's going to look you in the eye. She's going to tell you the true facts. The experts will describe their forensic examinations of her scarred body, of her scarred mind, and the experts will explain why she did not form the intent to kill."

I paused at this point to emphasize the nature of the abuse. I picked up the photos we had introduced to show her bruised body. I apologized to the jury for putting them through the trauma of viewing the pictures, then did exactly that.

"These photos reflect the terrible beatings at the hands of Betty's husband, Sam, but the photos do not begin to demonstrate the damage of his psychotic abuse of her mind.

"I'm sorry to talk about intimate details that would be best left undescribed in normal circumstances. Unfortunately, these are not normal circumstances or normal abuse. The truth about the depraved abuse in this case is required so that you can grasp why Betty could not and did not run, could not escape. The facts show why she believed, without question, that he planned to kill her daughter, Beth, and herself that morning."

I ticked off the coming proofs.

"Betty's account of the effect of that abuse on her actions will be supported by the expert testimony of Dr. Rob Willoby, a leading psychologist in Michigan whose practice is located here in town. Dr. Willoby has been called on for expert testimony for both the prosecution and defense in numerous cases. He does not take sides but gives his honest, expert opinion only. He has made an extensive examination of Betty and Beth and has worked with them both in therapy.

"Dr. Ben Deering will provide testimony of the horrible injuries suffered by Betty at the hands of Sam. He has completed an in-depth medical examination of the defendant. The technical evidence he'll present will be impossible to disregard. We will show you that Betty was not only in abject fear of Sam killing Beth that morning, but that she was so overcome by that fear she had no ability to intentionally premeditate a murder. Betty took the gun from under Sam's bed to make sure he would not use it against her, and as she stood there in abject fear for little Beth's life, the gun went off.

"Dr. Willoby will testify that her state of mind at that moment meets all the criteria for what is called temporary insanity by reason of irresistible impulse. He will also testify that Betty's Quaker beliefs against killing or injuring another human being prevented her from ever considering killing Sam, and that she now requires extensive therapy to learn how to face the death that happened in her presence.

I had to give enough explanation, but not too much, for the jury to start forming the logical story that would lead to acquittal.

"We know the gun went off. But no one has ever said why, and Betty has no idea why. Betty was incapacitated. She says she heard a sound in her head, and then the gun went off."

I leaned toward the jury. "Did Waterman awake and grab that gun and cause it to fire? Did Betty's hand unconsciously tighten on the gun and cause it to go off? Did something cause that gun to go off?

"When we talk about irresistible impulse, we are talking about something simple on its face. Irresistible means the thought or action is beyond a person's control. In other words, it cannot be stopped by the person in its grip.

"In this case, the testimony will show Betty was gripped by her certainty that her beloved child, Beth, was going to be killed that morning. Not just killed but killed in a terrible way. Sam throwing her into the furnace and burning her alive. The belief that Beth would be killed and the need to defend her was so powerful there was nothing Betty could think of but the horror inside her head, but certainly with no premeditation.

"The judge has told you that Michigan law requires the prosecutor prove all elements of a crime beyond a reasonable doubt. The judge will tell you more completely about the law when all the testimony is completed, and we have argued our view of the case to you. I am asking you to remember the body fluid found on that shotgun, the kitten remains found in the furnace, and the physical and mental evidence of abuse."

I held up three fingers. "There are three possible reasons that the gun went off – Waterman grabbed it, Betty unknowingly squeezed it, or something else intervened that is unknown.

"There is one speculative reason the gun went off, and that speculation is the prosecutor's unproven theory of premeditated murder. It is the prosecutor's burden to prove his theory of premeditation beyond a reasonable doubt. He cannot do so by speculating.

"I do not ask you to find her not guilty in spite of some small doubt. I will ask you to find her not guilty because all the evidence will say that she did not intend it, and it would have been against every fiber in her character to do so. There is no evidence she premeditated it or intended it. The prosecution theory is just that – a theory. And we do not convict innocent people on unproven theories."

I finished the way I always finished. I raised the jury's role up the flagpole.

"You know what the American flag looks like when it's waving."

It wasn't a question but me bonding to the jury using a shared image. "The jury system in America is the envy of the world. The willingness of Americans to give of their time to assume the burden of judging the facts in complex cases is unique to our ideal of justice.

"You have assumed that burden, and I thank you for it. Your willingness to assume such awesome responsibility gives me confidence that each of you will approach the evidence in this case with fairness and an open mind.

"My part in this case is not as a witness but as the one called to present Betty's defense in a complete and truthful manner. I will do the best I can to make sure the facts we present will be truthful statements of the defendant and her witnesses to the best their memories dictate. We will present physical evidence that will support Betty's truthfulness and innocence.

"I am confident the facts will demonstrate that Sam's death was not premeditated and was not intentional because, if Betty did anything at all, it was the result of an irresistible impulse."

That opening statement was what we call "a belt and suspenders" opening statement: She didn't do it, but if she did do it, she didn't intend to.

I concluded, "Thank you for your service," and I moved back to my chair.

As I started to sit down, I touched her shoulder, as I do every defendant, to show the jury I was with my client. In this case, Betty looked up with such adoration that I nearly regretted it. I would have to watch that. It was one thing to show solidarity with the client, but another thing altogether to show love.

O'Bannon had been sitting self-defensively and now he raised his eyes to watch me. As he did, I saw his attention fix on my copy of his investigation report, which I had discovered in the attorney conference room. His eyebrows shot up, and a sudden look of anger washed across his face.

It was exactly as I'd planned. I'd pulled the pin on O'Bannon's explosive personality by leaving the document in plain sight.

Betty would be my first witness, and I wanted O'Bannon to attack. That was what I'd prepared Betty for and hoped would come.

CHAPTER 30

Defense Strategy

I had discussed the trial strategy at length with Rob Willoby and Jim Drew. It was important to keep the case relatively simple in its presentation. We had to make our points succinctly and emphasize them several times. Our approach had to be simple and sophisticated at the same time.

I remembered the advice of the oldest trial attorney in our circuit, who won cases everyone else thought impossible. He took me aside after one of the trials I had lost and gave me some advice I took to heart.

"You gave the jury too much credit. You were so sure of your facts, you only stated them once to the jury. You have to repeat your points. Don't assume they understand it at first, even when you have made it plain. Deliver your point several times if it's important to your case."

We agreed that calling Betty first made the most sense. I was sure the jury would be deeply struck by Jerry's opening statement at the close of his proofs. They would have heard the worst of the case.

After Betty, we would call Shawn Roberts to establish the chain of possession of the shotgun, Ben Deering for his examination results of Betty, and, perhaps, reputation witnesses of Betty, if needed. Rob Willoby would follow to report on Betty's psychological exam.

Depending on how effectively our proofs were proceeding, we could call Sam's friends, who Jim recorded on tape. With any luck at all, we would not need to call any of them.

Jerry had listed Ira Waterman, and we had listed Ira and Evelyn Waterman, his wife, as Sam's parents. I was sure they would never reach the stand although Jim had found Ira extraordinarily boastful and cross-examining him would be a bonus for the defense.

CHAPTER 31

Betty Testifies

I **smiled to look confident,** but inside I felt the familiar dread I felt anytime I called a client. Betty was prepared, and the table was laid, as they say. But a criminal defendant is the whole case, and the trial lawyer's obsessive fear of losing control is heightened by the knowledge that O'Bannon was ready to tear Betty to pieces in front of the jury.

We needed her to establish the foundation for the rest of our witness list. She was the only person who could describe what life was like in the house where her husband died. That's what a trial attorney must do: The head must convince the nerves "this is necessary, so I will do it."

My voice was artificially steady. "The defense calls Betty Waterman, Your Honor," I said.

A courtroom is designed so witnesses testify close to the jury. The body language, the sound of the voice, the eye movements – the jury can pick it all up. The judge's bench is always raised, like an altar. The witness box is right next to the bench – in this case, it was on the left – and the jury box was three feet from it.

I began my direct exam with the required questions for the record – name, address, status as defendant.

My voice was a little louder than normal to remind her to project hers to the whole jury. Then I went right to it.

"Did you shoot Sam Waterman on purpose?" I asked. Her eyes widened, as we'd discussed, in response to what was an unsettling question. Her face otherwise was calm and composed.

"I don't know. I was holding the gun and I heard something like a scream in my head, and it went off, and I saw all the blood on the bed. It was ..." and her face showed dismay.

That was it, exactly what was in the police report on the date of the incident, with just enough difference to sound genuine and unrehearsed.

I asked her to tell me about the hours leading up to the incident.

She took a deep breath. "The night before, Sam was in a rage. There was no reason I could see why he was so angry. He said he hated the dinner I made and threw it in my face. He was angry that the dinner dishes weren't washed. I knew that wasn't the reason because he ordered me to go to his bed while I was still rinsing the plates."

The way she said "made me go to his bed" sounded like a dog being ordered to go to its crate. I interrupted softly. "What does that mean?"

She said, "An order," and shrugged slightly. It was a key point to show she was not in control. I motioned for her to go on.

"There was a cot I used in Beth's room, but he would threaten me when I tried to stay away from him. When he ordered me to, I'd get into his bed and he would do things." The courtroom was deadly silent.

"What things?" It was hurtful but necessary.

"I mean, you know, rape me and things." Her head hung in embarrassment. She didn't look up. "If I didn't let him, he'd threaten to kill both of us." She looked at the jury. "Beth and me. Beth is three years old. He swore he would hurt her badly."

I prompted her. "Tell the jury specifically what happened the night before the incident."

She looked at the jury, who were unblinking. "That night he was different. He struck me in the face hard with his fist. Usually he'd avoid bruising my face, because people would see the bruises, but this time it seemed he wanted to hurt my face. I was confused at first because it was different this time, and then I knew. He wasn't worried. Beth was screaming, and it seemed for a moment he was going to hit her, too. But then he forgot her and raped me, like it had excited him to hit my face."

I was having trouble keeping my voice even. My throat seemed to be closing. An attorney wants to stay out of the way of testimony like this, so I did just that. I just nodded and gestured for her to continue.

"He pulled his shotgun from under the bed and jammed the gun barrel into my vagina, and said it had a hair trigger, and then laughed like it was a joke. He said he was going to kill me and Beth then and there if I didn't have sex with him. He'd said that before, and I always did what he wanted. But that night, using force on me was what he wanted. I had to protect her, so I just laid there while he did it."

The tension from the women in the jury box was almost palpable. I felt my legs going numb from being locked in place, and I shifted my stance.

"That night, when he finished, he grabbed me by my hair and held my face close to his. He said he was going to kill me and Beth in the morning. He said he was done having to beg for sex."

She looked at the jury, sharing her own horror. "He said he had a woman who would perform a lot better, 'a hell of a lot better,' he said, and he was sick and tired of having Beth and me around. He said he would take care of her just like the kitten."

Then she lost everything. She choked and her body began to shake uncontrollably. Tears ran down her cheeks. She fumbled for a tissue, but her hands danced erratically in the air above the tissue, unable to grasp it.

"Tell the jury about the furnace," I said.

"Just two days before that night, he'd forced me to open the door on the furnace. He held the kitten up in one hand, then threw it into the flames. I remember screaming before I fainted. I woke up lying on the bed. He had stripped me naked and was on top of me, raping me. When he finished, I was sick to my stomach. The sound that kitten made ...

"The night before he died. I knew it was different. We'd tried to escape before, and it only made it worse. I sat up all night holding Beth. I rocked her all night trying to figure something out. She is everything to me!" It came out in a scream that was muffled by her hands.

"You have to understand he was fanatical about giving his word. He said he was going to kill us the next morning. He bragged that he always did what he had promised, no matter what. He'd rather lose a fistfight or take a beating than back down.

"That night, when he said he'd kill both of us in the morning, I was terrified. He had never said that. I knew without a shadow of a doubt that he really did intend to kill me and Beth in the morning, and if we tried to run it would be no use. It just was worse when he brought us back home."

She tried to explain. "You wouldn't think there could be something worse than yourself dying, but ..." It was clear she was thinking of Beth.

She stopped and looked at me, coming out of her own thoughts. "What did you ask me?"

The trauma of telling the story was wearing her down fast. Emotional exhaustion is a real problem. I had to leave her something so she could withstand O'Bannon when he crossed her.

I gave her a moment as I walked to our counsel table and retrieved the photographs of Betty that I'd taken in my office. They were marked as Defense Exhibit A. After asking the judge's permission, I passed them out to the jury.

One by one, the emotions on the jurors' faces became palpable as the photos were passed. Several of the women jurors were openly in tears, and more than one of the men had veins standing out on their forehead. If Sam had been there, he would have had to defend himself from a hell of a beating.

"Describe what happened in the morning," I said.

"I hadn't slept," she said. "I dressed Beth and went into his bedroom to tell him I would be a good wife to him. I was going to say I loved him and didn't want him to go to jail for killing us. I was going to say that if he let Beth go to my parents, I would do anything he wanted and would never again complain, that he could go ahead with his other woman.

"Then as I stood beside the bed, everything just flooded my brain. Blood was running down my leg from the shotgun the night before. It seemed at that moment there was nothing else in the room. It seemed the walls were moving in. The shotgun was sticking out from just under the edge of the mattress. It seemed so dangerous. I touched it, and then I picked it up. I wanted to make sure he couldn't reach it when he woke and kill Beth. It was cold and heavy. I'd never had it in my hands before but watched him play with it so many times when he assaulted me."

I stopped her for a point. "Had you ever shot the gun before?" I asked.

"No, I don't know how," she said meekly.

"But you'd seen him handle it, play with it?" I asked.

"Yes, he teased me with it, said it had a hair trigger. I never knew what that meant. I thought he was making a joke about what he did to me."

"Tell the jury what happened next," I said.

"And then I saw a picture of him in my mind approaching

the open doors of the furnace with Beth screaming in his arms. It was so clear, it seemed to be happening in front of me. All I could think was, oh God, no! I don't know what happened then, don't have a memory of anything, but I heard an explosion. Then I looked down and he was dead on the bed."

Her shoulders slumped, and I actually felt the agony of that moment. The jury was transfixed, immobile and intent.

I waited and then she went on. "It took some time, I couldn't believe it," she said, "and then I felt so badly and couldn't figure out what to do. I'm a Quaker, and it's a sin to kill or injure another human."

"Tell the jury about coming to my office that morning," I said.

"I felt so guilty I could hardly walk. I called my mother to pick up Beth, waited for her on the front porch, and then walked to your office." She shrugged. "You were the only one I thought of who would know what to do."

I thought grimly, "So much for hiding our relationship" but put the thought aside.

"Betty, did you premeditate the murder of your husband?" I asked the question for the record.

"Never, never," she said, shaking her head.

"When you walked into his bedroom, did you plan to find the gun and shoot him?"

"No, of course not. That is a mortal sin and I never would have done that," she answered. "I had never thought of killing him despite despising him for everything. Never, in my wildest dreams did I ever think to kill him. That's something I would never do, and that's why it took some time to realize that I must have pulled that trigger."

"Did you pull the trigger?" I had to ask.

"I don't know!" she raised her voice. "I wish I did – it would make this easier!"

"Betty, I'm going to leave that line of questioning now. I want you to follow my next question. When you returned to your house on the day of the incident, did you notice anything unusual?"

"Yes, while I was there, a blue Chevy two-door drove up around noon. The driver stopped in front of the house for a time and then left. I wrote down the first three letters on the license, HBV, but I couldn't see the driver's face. I thought it might be the other woman, Sam's girlfriend, but I didn't know."

"I have one more question, Mrs. Waterman. How long did you speak with Dr. Arti Brown during his psychological evaluation?"

"Not long," she said. "He was in a hurry. I would say he was there less than ten minutes."

"Thank you." I picked my notes off the lectern and spoke to O'Bannon. "Your witness," I said.

CHAPTER 32

Prosecution Cross of Betty

O'Bannon came out of his chair like a projectile aimed at Betty and stopped only a few feet in front of her. He was bristling, puffed up like a fighting cock ready for battle – just as I'd hoped he would be.

In his first question to Betty, he threw caution to the wind.

"Are you aware that Michigan does not recognize a husband's assaulting his wife to enforce marital sex as rape?" he asked.

"Objection!" I said. "The prosecution is misstating the law. Michigan does not fail to recognize a husband's forcing sex as rape; it only decriminalizes the act by a husband."

Judge Blevin had seen it coming as well as I. "Sustained," he said quickly.

O'Bannon spun and glared at me for effect before continuing.

"You have called your very own husband's sexual conduct rape. Wasn't he simply enforcing his rights in the marriage, his entitlement of service from his wife? Why do you continue to call that legal action rape?"

The trap was sprung. Our ambush had worked. Jerry's anger had led him into that fabled area where angels fear to tread. It was the question we had prepared for, and Betty's answer would be the core of our defense.

Her eyes were up now, looking at him directly, no weakness. She cleared her throat.

"There was nothing simple or normal in Sam's demands for sex," she said. "He told me later he'd drugged and raped me the first night I met him, the night at the bar when I blacked out, before we were ever married and before I ever consented to anything more than a beer with him.

"After I learned I was pregnant and was married to him, that's when he told me everything. He enjoyed telling me he took me home and raped me while I was unconscious. A short time after that, I told him we were through, and I wanted a divorce. He told me to wait and he would talk about it. He said Beth would have a last name. Then, after she was born and I told him I still wanted a divorce, he slugged me in the stomach for the first time, as hard as he could, and told me that Beth and I would both be dead the same day I saw a lawyer."

She choked up and her tears came fast. She turned to the jury and pulled herself together. She clenched her hands on the chair arms for support before continuing in a much quieter voice.

O'Bannon tried to talk over her, but Blevin waved him off. "Let her finish her answer," he said.

"I was totally unprepared for him. He would rip my pants off and shove that shotgun barrel into my vagina and move it. He'd say, 'Do you want me to pull the trigger or are you ready for what I want?' I would beg him to stop. He would move the barrel in my vagina. Do you know there is a metal sight on the top of the barrel, Mr. O'Bannon?"

She waited for him to answer, and she suddenly realized her newfound power.

"I screamed, Mr. O'Bannon, and he climbed on top of me

and raped me where I was cut." She was now completely in control, and her strength filled her voice in the courtroom.

Each sentence was engraved. "He thought that was fun. He did it when he wanted and how he wanted. He'd pull that shotgun out from under the mattress, put the barrel up against my vagina and ask the same question each time: 'You want to fight or fuck?' And then he'd say, 'Never bring a pussy to a gunfight.'"

She addressed the jury, "I'm sorry. The words are so foul, but that's what it was like."

She turned back to O'Bannon. "He yelled about 'Nichols' and high school. I tried to convince him I hadn't talked or met Robert in years without him being there too, but it was no use."

O'Bannon took the opportunity to make another accusation posed as a question.

"Mrs. Waterman, do you admit your husband was defenseless as you stood over him in bed?" He looked at the jury, a hint of a satisfied smile.

"No," she said. I had told her to play it very straight, answer the question as simply as possible. She wouldn't follow him on this one.

"He was asleep, on his back, unaware you were in the room," O'Bannon pressed her.

"Some of that is true, some I don't know." She looked at him, waiting for the next.

O'Bannon was obviously trying to parse her answer. He couldn't because he hadn't really been listening. He'd been waiting to ask his next question. He made the wrong decision and asked her an open-ended question that opened the door again. "What does that mean?"

I didn't know if she knew the difference between an open door and a leading question, but she took his question and beat him over the head with it.

"He raped me at least twice a week for most of the three years since Beth was born. He would go as long as a month even if I did as little as I could to provoke him. There were times I'd think he was asleep in a chair or his bed, and I'd try to sneak away, and suddenly he'd grab me and force me. He'd just hurt me for sport.

"You ask whether he was asleep that morning. Who knows? He did things to trick me all the time, then hurt me. All I knew was his threats were real. I lived in constant danger and whenever I started to think of a way out, he seemed to have an animal sense and would spring something new.

"During this past year he came up with some new tricks. He would rape me while little Beth watched. You know, she was only three, so I hope she didn't understand. When he hurt me, I tried to be quiet and not upset Beth.

"But he liked scaring her. That morning, I don't know if he was asleep or faking. I just don't know. But it wouldn't have been the first time he'd faked being unconscious and then done something bad."

Suddenly I was on full alert again. I had never heard that. It fit with the idle notion I'd introduced that Waterman had been awake and tried to grab the gun, causing it to discharge.

Betty was just going with the open-ended question she'd been asked, unaware she'd opened a new point of attack.

"He loved scaring us when we let down our guard. Beth's usual hiding place is behind her old crib in my room, and I'd sit with her and hold her. Sam would turn off the overhead light, and crawl in the dark, and then jump up and yell. Can you imagine, Mr. O'Bannon, a man like that?"

Betty was nearly spent. The picture of the little girl being forced to watch her mother being raped, the thought of a grown man intentionally terrorizing a child. It all was too hard to grasp.

"He had hurt me and told me he was going to kill me and Beth in the morning. Then he went to bed. The next morning, was he waiting for me to come into his bedroom? Was he going to scare us to death? Did he wait and then grab the gun from me? I don't know because I was so upset, I have no memory. Did he grab that gun? I wouldn't put that past him for a second."

She knew where she was now with O'Bannon. She didn't show it, but I could tell. She knew she could say it and have it stick to him. "You tell me what that man did that morning."

It was a risky thing for a defendant to challenge an experienced prosecutor. But the way she did it, it had a ring of truth, a ring of sincerity.

"I stood there ready to sacrifice the rest of my life if he would let my little girl go. Then the gun went off. Really, that's all I know of that moment, except this – murder was against everything I've ever believed in and lived. That was not what happened. Something else happened, and I won't pretend to tell the jury what it was," and she looked straight along the jury box, as she said, "You ask me what I mean, and that is what I mean."

O'Bannon objected and asked to strike defendant's answer as unresponsive.

"To the contrary," Judge Blevin responded. "You asked what she meant and she answered the question. The defendant's answer will stand as directly responsive to your question. I suggest you move on."

"Move on I shall," said Jerry, seething. It was starkly obvious in the courtroom that he was at war with the judge. It was the stupidest possible mistake any lawyer could make.

He tried to go after her. "Betty, you are also claiming self-defense. Was there anyone in your home preventing you from leaving with your daughter, Beth, either the night before or that morning before pulling the trigger?"

"Yes." Nice and simple.

"Didn't you have a car to drive away in? Did you or did you not have the ability to leave the premises without killing Sam?" O'Bannon asked.

"There was a car and a door," she said.

He hesitated, as if he would try to control her, then moved on. "You are also claiming 'irresistible impulse.' Are you really claiming you could not stop yourself from killing Sam?"

"I was not aware of doing whatever I did. Yes, that is exactly right," she said. "I still find it difficult to believe that I killed him, but I have no explanation for how that gun went off. I only remember that sound in my head when I thought about him putting Beth in the furnace, and then I heard the explosion. He was dead and the gun was in my hands."

Bloody but unbowed, O'Bannon was boxed in by his lack of preparation. He came at her again, hoping he'd find a crack in her concentration.

"Do you expect this jury to believe Sam would announce his intention to kill you and Beth and then calmly go to sleep in the house with you there? You are lying, are you not?"

She smiled almost to herself, and in that moment, I saw the woman I had fallen in love with. She was so tired, so spent, that her composure had a surreal calm.

"Everything I have told you is the truth," she said. "I don't think I have changed my story from the moment I spoke with the police. I am a Quaker, and my own fallibility is now a concern for my eternal soul. If I've said something false here, I will have to answer to greater authority than you. I mean no disrespect in any way to you, but if you ask me whether I am lying, I can assure you I am not."

There are virtuoso talents in any field. Betty, after all she had been through, had just shown a virtuosity for the truth.

O'Bannon checked his notes. He sneered at her. He sneered in my general direction, as if I were somehow complicit. Then he stalked back to his seat.

"I'm done with this witness," he said without looking at Judge Blevin to whom the remark had been addressed. It was a crude form of disrespect to a witness who had defeated him with rectitude.

I stood up for redirect.

"Do you recall when the prosecutor told you rape was legal for a husband?"

"Yes," she said.

"And you recall the prosecutor said rape by a husband – even with a shotgun – is legal?" I nodded for her to answer.

"Yes, I do," she said.

"Now tell me, when you picked up that shotgun that morning, were you going to kill Sam because he raped you?"

She hit it perfectly. "I had been raped so many times by my husband that at that point I was not even thinking of that."

"If you were not thinking about being raped, what then were you thinking about?"

"I was," and she sobbed, "only thinking of Beth being shoved into that furnace, screaming, terrified as she caught on fire."

"So Betty, when you picked up that shotgun and you had that vision of Beth, what happened next?"

"I suddenly heard a sound in my head like 'Oh God, nooooo!' and suddenly there was an explosion and I looked down and he was horrible ...,"

"Do you know what caused that shotgun to go off?"

"No, I didn't aim or think about it or intend to shoot it." Her head shook slightly, as if subtly puzzling over what had happened.

"No further questions," I said.

Judges listen to important testimony. A neighbor fence dispute, not so much. A barking dog, not so much. A baseball going through a picture window, not. This was a first-degree murder case with gripping testimony by a woman who had been terrorized and brutalized for years before a grisly shooting.

Judge Blevin was listening. And he was not happy with the disrespectful treatment of a witness who had obviously tried to cooperate with police, with attorneys, and with the prosecutor who was trying to put her in prison for life.

The joy of dealing with O'Bannon had gone out of Judge Blevin's life, and he took the opportunity now to rebalance respect in his court.

He said in a very respectful voice, "Mrs. Waterman, I would like to thank you. You may return to your attorney's table now." He said it simply, but tellingly. He could not have made it clearer that he was thanking her for truthful testimony.

The bailiff came to help her back to the counsel table. She managed to stand, clutched his arm and walked very slowly to her chair.

I could have hugged her. I should have hugged her.

It was 4:30 at that point, and I asked for a recess. The court approved, and we assembled in the attorney's room to assess the testimony so far. Day #2 had gone well.

We had survived voir dire, openings, the prosecution's witnesses, and the defendant's cross-exam. That's all we hope for in criminal defense: survival.

••

As we sat there the bailiff knocked on the door to tell me that a witness wanted to see me urgently. He brought her in, and to my surprise, it was Evelyn Waterman, Sam's mother, who came in trembling and with tears on her cheeks. She was dressed in a loosely hanging sack-like house dress and I remembered Jim's description of her cowering in the living room of her home when he talked with Ira. His description fit her current look. She was clearly uncomfortable when I asked her to sit with us and tell us why it was urgent to see me. Her story poured out in a rush.

"I believe Ira intends to kill me and has intended to kill me since I was sitting in my own home the day before Sam was killed. That's when Sam told his dad that the next day was the 'big day.' I am now the only living witness and a danger to Ira."

She made it plain she was ready to testify and would

hold nothing back. Her fear of Ira and disgust with Sam were apparent. She embraced Betty fervently with tears flowing and begged her forgiveness for having taken so long to tell us.

I made a reservation for Evelyn in the best hotel in Pontiac, and one of Jim's assistants personally delivered her there. I told her not to call anyone or make contact of any kind with anyone to prevent Ira from finding her. Jim provided one of his assistants to guard her there, and she seemed very grateful. I asked if she needed money to tide her over, and she indicated she had saved a couple of hundred dollars over a long period of time and was able to get along for a time.

Jim left immediately to begin an investigation of Elsa's blue car and the Wick's Lumberyard purchase of plastic that Evelyn had just told us about. We had all gone from feeling good about Betty's performance to sky high with Evelyn's story. Her testimony was going to turn Jerry's slam dunk into a case with serious problems, and I knew the jury was going to be shocked beyond measure.

Talk about a hand grenade! This was going to blow Jerry out of his shorts. I realized this was one of those occasions when luck trumped skill. Betty had just gotten the next-to-last piece of the puzzle, although we all knew Jerry's expert would be the last piece and posed the biggest hurdle. Dr. Brown would testify that she was lying, and we had to give the jury enough to question the doctor's own truthfulness.

I sat with Betty for a few minutes after the others left and indicated we had a better chance now than at any time before, but still there were no guarantees. There was no way to hide the elation we felt at this new, promised testimony. We had no way to know if Evelyn could hold up in the face of her husband's threats. Ira had abused her for thirty years, and she would have to face Jerry's cross-exam of any testimony she gave. We would still have Dr. Brown to deal with, but if my estimate of his normal lack of preparation were correct, Jim's investigation gave us a path for an effective cross-examination.

Betty was happier than I had seen her since her first day in my office, and I had to agree Evelyn could be a huge help if she could stand up to Jerry's certain attack. If she could, our defense of truth was going to be substantially strengthened. When the bailiff came for her, Betty was a new woman. Her smile made my day.

CHAPTER 33

Defense Calls Evelyn, Shawn and Ben

The next day I called **Evelyn Waterman** to the stand as our first witness for the day. She was waiting in one of the attorney's rooms in the courthouse, and Jerry did a double take when he saw her walk into court. She was the first surprise in the trial, and he scrambled to find and read my witness list to make sure she was there. I was sure he had dismissed her name in his mind as a witness and was surprised to see that, sure as hell, her name was there.

His face fell, as I knew it would, because her name and Ira's were there in black and white. O'Bannon shrugged. In his mind, this frail, elderly woman probably had nothing to say. In any case, there was no way he could stop me from using her.

As Evelyn took the stand, she shed any resemblance to the cowering and beaten-down wife I'd interviewed. She raised her head and squared her jaw. Someone had given or loaned her a rose-colored dress, and it contrasted well with her neatly combed white hair. She looked at the jury and smiled. In an un-coachable way, she projected the confidence of a witness prepared to say her piece.

If you've seen enough trial witnesses, you can tell how they're going to do before they even start speaking. When they walk up to the witness box to be sworn in, they just have an aura. A surgeon friend once told me that he would meet every patient before an operation and put his hand on their head. He could tell which patient would have the best surgical result, just by the sense he got from that simple contact.

Evelyn raised her hand for the oath and said, "I do" in a voice that was steady and clear.

I asked her to identify herself and asked her to explain how she came to me the prior evening.

"I was a witness to my son Sam's plan to kill Betty and Beth, and I figured you ought to know about it," she answered.

"Have you been paid or promised anything for your testimony?" I asked.

"No. I came to you on my own," she said. "I never talked with you or anyone before yesterday."

"Why did you come forward now?" I asked.

She took a breath. "I've been scared. But I believe my husband, Ira, wants to kill me because of what I know," she said.

She gestured in Betty's direction, "I'm sorry for her. I waited too long. But I know in my heart this has to be said, and all this has to stop." Her hands fidgeted nervously with a seam of her dress, but her composure was good, direct, and I wanted to get her to transmit that to the jury.

"Will you please tell the jury what you mean when you say, 'All this has to stop.'?" I hoped she would take the prompt.

She did. She turned to the juror nearest her. "I heard the details of Sam and Ira's plan to kill Betty and Beth," she said. "Ever since then, Ira has warned me to say nothing. He said what would happen if I did."

"Tell the jury what that was," I said.

She looked at the juror again, hesitated only for the briefest instant, and then blurted, "I'm a dead woman if I talk!"

It was the second time the courtroom had been stunned in the space of three days. It was an electric moment, the kind that anneals a jury together like the hardest steel.

"Could you tell us, in your own words, exactly what you heard Sam and Ira planning?" I wanted to step completely out of the way of her testimony. I added, "Please tell the jury."

She swiveled completely in the witness chair toward the jury. "I was in the side room of our place on October third of last year, the day before Sam was killed. And I," and she caught her breath, and then said softly, "You know, even after all the things he did, he was still my flesh and blood."

She looked down, then raised her eyes again. "Sam was telling Ira how he would do it the next day. Ira was saying what he could do to help. They were being loud. I just sat there quiet. I couldn't say anything or Ira would have done something to me then."

Her composure finally broke at that point and she searched in her dress pocket for a tissue, out of habit apparently, but this dress had no pocket. "The apple didn't fall far," she said, and shook her head sadly.

Judge Blevin made a gesture, and the bailiff handed Evelyn a box of tissues. She smiled the most defeated, grateful smile I had ever seen. It was as if that box of tissues were the first male human kindness she had ever known.

When she did that, she was still facing the jury, courtesy

of the bailiff's positioning of the tissue box. As he returned to his chair by the opposite door, he gave me a wink that only I could see. A bailiff's wink is like a landslide political survey.

I asked, "Are you okay to continue?" and she nodded, and I said, "Then please continue."

She turned to me to answer, away from the jury, but now that was unnecessary. They knew who and what she was, and more eye contact wasn't important.

"It started when Sam came to the house after work at about 5:30 p.m. and told Ira that the next day was the big day," she said. "He went on about Betty, called her names, said how the little brat's screaming and crying was irritating, said the sight of his gun made her start screaming, and I knew what he meant because of what he did with the gun. He learned that from his dad." She hesitated, then blurted, "I don't put up with that anymore." She held her head up, but her face was still embarrassed at her disclosure.

"Even though Sam was my son, that man was bad through and through. He hated his own wife and child. Same way as Ira. It was sick the way those two treated women. Sam said how he and Elsa would be together soon.

"He told Ira he would be cleaning up his problems the next day so he and Elsa could finally live together." She shook her head, clearly disgusted.

I pressed her about the murder plan. "Can you recall any details about how Sam planned to kill Beth and Betty?"

She said, "He said he had bought Betty a used car a week before, and made Betty drive it with Beth in a car seat. He'd send her out on errands in the car, so she'd be seen in the car with Beth, normal like. Everyone in town would see her out, would think she could go anywhere she wanted.

"Then he asked Ira to make sure his backhoe would be at the Turner barn job site the next day. Ira told him okay, no problem. He even volunteered to dig an extra-deep hole where they were getting ready to erect the barn. He said they'd be eight feet under before the cement floor was poured.

"Joe Stone was scheduled to do the floor the day after, but he didn't know anything about the murders. Ira said the police would be looking for Betty and the brat as runaways, and no one would ever be the wiser."

She began to shudder, and I asked the court for a few minutes of recess. Judge Blevin quickly obliged. I purposefully kept my distance during the break. O'Bannon was watching me. When Evelyn took the stand ten minutes later, I simply asked her to continue her story.

"Ira approved the plan, which shocked me. I knew he had it in him, but it didn't seem real. Ira didn't even hesitate. All he was interested in was to make sure Sam thought of everything. He asked Sam what he planned to do with Betty's car after he disposed of the bodies. Sam said he would drive it north of Bay City to a wooded site he knew and burn it. Elsa had bought a five-gallon gas can. Then Elsa could drive him home in her own car. Ira even offered to drive Betty's car north so Sam would have an alibi of being on the job all day, but Sam said he didn't need Ira's help.

"Sam said he planned to choke them both to death to avoid blood evidence. The plan was for Elsa to come to the house at noon. They'd load the bodies together in the trunk of her car wrapped in plastic, just in case, and they'd both drive over to the job site. He said Elsa had bought plastic sheeting from Wick's in Bay City so no one could trace it locally.

"After they got back from burning the car near Bay City, Sam would pretend that Betty and Beth were missing and call around to the police.

"He said everyone would question where they'd gone, but he had a story planned. He'd tell her family there'd been a lot of fighting in the marriage, and he'd asked for a divorce, and Betty was so mad she threatened to take Beth and leave him for good. She was angry and left in the morning of the fourth without saying where she and Beth were headed. He'd say he expected her to blow off steam and then come back, but she never came home."

As Evelyn described the murder plan, I was watching the jury, and they were mesmerized. Evelyn spoke with an unnerving calmness. She was tired, defeated, and utterly truthful. I wondered how O'Bannon would approach her.

I had a few last small points to wrap up. "Did Ira ever try to talk Sam out of it?" I asked.

"Never," she said. "In fact, it was Ira's company that was doing the Turner barn job. He came up with the idea of the backhoe and burying them under the concrete slab."

"Did you attempt to warn Betty or the police?" I asked.

That stopped her. She shook her head. She said she'd started to leave that night, but when she tried to go outside, Ira grabbed her and dragged her back into the house and smacked her.

"I think those men had that in common. Talk of violence, I think it excited them," she said. "Anyway, I didn't because I couldn't. I was too afraid, too used to all of it. I don't know, you just get beat down to where you just can't do anything." She looked at the jurors. "They almost did it. I'm sorry," she said, and then looked straight at Betty.

"In a strange way, I feel like it actually happened because when I woke up on the morning of the fourth, I was sure Sam had already killed them. I can remember what it felt like knowing that Betty and Beth were dead. When I heard Sam was the one dead, I said, "Thank God!"

She looked down. "Isn't that horrible? I hear my son has died, and I say, 'Thank God'?" She looked up. "Can you imagine?"

I had to answer her. I said I couldn't. The jury nodded.

"Anyway, the day Sam died, Elsa called just after noon. She was yelling into the phone so loud that Ira had to hold it away from his ear. She said there were a bunch of police cars at Sam's place, and Sam hadn't come out to meet her when she drove up in front of the house. Something must have gone wrong, so she drove away. She didn't know what to do now.

"Ira called the police and that's when we learned that Betty shot him. That's when I said 'Thank God.' Then Ira slapped me so hard he knocked me to the floor. I thought he was going to kill me right then and there. He called Elsa to tell her, and I could hear her screaming Betty's name and how she would kill that murdering bitch.

"He knew that I'd heard it all. That's when I got scared – and more scared with each passing day. I've never been more terrified in my life." Her eyes were full again, and she was drained.

I turned and said, "Your witness."

O'Bannon had a mess on his hands. An unexpected witness, shocking testimony, a rapt jury, tears that seemed unlikely to stop.

He did the only thing an unprepared blusterer does when he's cornered. He started his cross-exam with a direct attack.

"What have you been offered to tell this incredible story in court?" he asked.

She looked at him and said, "What did you say?"

"I said who offered you what to lie to this jury?" he said, blustering.

"Nobody offered me nothing. Well, they said they'd protect me from Ira," she answered. "I asked Mr. Nichols to help me get a divorce from Ira, but he said it would be a conflict or something like that. A friend of his guarded my room last night, if that's what you're interested in."

"And how long did he spend practicing your testimony?" O'Bannon sneered, looking at the jury, expecting a good answer.

"What do you mean?" she said.

"You know exactly what I mean. I mean how many hours did Mr. Nichols spend with you practicing your testimony? How many suggestions did he make in the way you should look at the jury, and with tears in your eyes?" He was breathing audibly, leaning forward on the podium aggressively.

"You don't understand. I told him what I knew. He listened for a couple minutes and then asked about my well-being and called a friend to stand guard outside my room in case Ira found out where I was. That's all. He didn't tell me anything." She had a look that truly conveyed she wasn't sure what O'Bannon meant by his insinuations.

O'Bannon tried one more time, asking if she meant the jury to believe I hadn't coached her or given her money for her motel room.

She got it that time. "I'd been saving for several years, and I had saved $200 to escape that man. But if you're thinking someone paid me to tell a story that may get me killed, you're mistaken, sir."

It was a clean kill. O'Bannon could not even put a game face on. He pretended to look at his notes, then stammered, "No further questions."

I quickly asked Judge Blevin to approach the bench, and he waved us both forward. "Your Honor, I am requesting the court direct the sheriff's department to take Mrs. Waterman into protective custody until her husband can be detained on charges of attempted murder."

Judge Blevin looked at O'Bannon for comment. There was nothing to say, but he tried anyway. "Judge, this is all a bunch of malarkey."

Judge Blevin interrupted. "If you don't lower your voice, I'm going to raise mine." He had his hand over his microphone, and he exhaled. "Clear?" he asked him, and O'Bannon simply nodded.

Blevin motioned to the bailiff, who joined us at the bench.

"Sergeant, I want you to direct the sheriff to assist Mrs. Waterman into protective custody. I want it to be safe, and I want it to be comfortable. I want it on the county's bill, understood?"

The bailiff knew exactly what was going on, and something told me the jury did too.

"Gentlemen, you can return to counsel table, and we will proceed until the noon break."

I called Shawn Roberts, my first expert witness and after establishing his status as an expert, started with the routine foundation questions.

He got to the point quickly. "I am here because you asked our laboratory to test the weapon on the counsel table," he said. "We are the state's leading biologic testing lab, and the testing you requested was our certified area of special expertise. We tested the barrel of the gun and found vaginal fluid residue and dried blood to a depth of eight inches from the tip of the barrel. We confirmed the identity of the fluids with lab tests, and ascertained, with one hundred percent confidence that the fluids match that of the defendant, Betty Waterman."

It would be an overstatement to say the jury had already heard so much troubling testimony that they were numbed. I wanted to imprint the scientific identification.

"Can you explain the methodology of your testing?" I asked.

He was wearing a white shirt with a pocket envelope of pens, like an engineer. He was a perfect science nerd.

"Since 1953 when the human genome was deciphered, there has been the potential for DNA matching. Our laboratory has been on the leading edge of this breakthrough science in Michigan. We are the only laboratory capable of this type of precise matching in the state at this time."

I asked, "I understand the gun was brought to your laboratory in a soft gun case," I said. "Did you also test fluids from that case?"

"Yes. In forensic terms, that test was not conclusive. We swabbed the case and found very minimal residue. There was no indication of a sufficient quantity of fluid to be the source for either the vaginal fluid or the blood that we found on the gun barrel. The only thing we could reliably conclude was that the residue in the case came from the gun, not the other way around."

I offered the laboratory report as defendant's Exhibit B and passed the witness to O'Bannon. It was a tough one for him, because O'Bannon routinely relied on Roberts in prosecution cases, and if he damaged Roberts's reputation or his lab's reputation, he would be alienating an important ally. He elected not to cross-examine.

After the jury examined the biologics report, I called Dr. Ben Deering to the witness stand. After the foundational questions, I addressed the extensive physical examination he'd done on Betty.

"Were you able to determine whether there were injuries to the vaginal region?" I asked.

"Yes, I did. I also furnished a blood sample to Mr. Roberts's laboratory for comparison of the DNA."

"To a reasonable degree of scientific certainty, what were your findings?" I asked, using the required legal language of probability.

"I found severe, permanent scarring and some callousing of the vaginal canal. From the size and progression, it appeared to be the product of repeated contacts with a blunt instrument having a projection. There was evidence of scars from small lacerations. There was a fairly large scabbing from an insult that would have occurred within two weeks of the examination.

"I examined photographs of the barrel end of the shotgun allegedly used by Sam Waterman to threaten and abuse Betty Waterman. I can state with a high degree of likelihood the scars and scab were consistent with the size, material, and components of the gun barrel with a projecting sight, such as I reviewed on the subject shotgun.

"Based on the biologic lab results, and my examination of both the victim's anatomy and the barrel, it is my opinion that Betty Waterman was subjected to assault with that shotgun barrel multiple times. The measurement of six inches of the barrel demonstrating residual vaginal fluid and blood is consistent with the depth of Betty's injuries I found and also was the fundamental cause of the seriousness of her injuries."

"Were the injuries substantial or superficial?" I asked.

"The damage is significant and permanent. She will require reconstructive surgery with no guarantee that she will ever be able to have normal relations pain-free. This type of surgery has a success rate of about sixty percent."

O'Bannon was on his feet to object. "I object, Your Honor, because residual injury – or any injury – is completely irrelevant to the issues in this case."

Judge Blevin arched his eyebrow at me for a reply.

"Your Honor, the damage clearly goes to state of mind, which *is* an issue in the defendant's irresistible impulse defense, and also to her veracity. Finally, it is relevant for the same reason the biologics lab found it relevant." The last point was a stretch, because I had initiated the lab tests, but I thought mention of it fit the moment.

Blevin had to err on the side of a defendant in a premeditated murder case with high potential penalties. It was not a hard call. His voice was measured, but he said, "Objection overruled on one or more of the bases cited by the defense."

I indicated Deering could continue. "I will take your opinion about surgical probability, if you recall my question."

Deering said, "Without surgery, Betty will face the emotional and physical trauma of persistent vaginal pain upon contact. There is also a likelihood that, if she had any wish to bear another child, it would be difficult, painful, and most likely, unsuccessful."

To put a point on it, Dr. Deering looked at the jury and shook his head slightly, as if to say, 'Those are the scientific results, sorry.'

"Have you seen injuries of this nature and magnitude caused by any customary, non-assaultive method in your career?" I asked.

"No," he looked at the jury. "These examination results are a type that I have seen only in sexual assault victims – those who suffered assault by foreign objects. I should also add that I have never seen injuries this severe."

On my request, he handed his report to me and said, "I have made a complete report with photographs, measurements and laboratory data."

I offered it, and Judge Blevin admitted Deering's report as Exhibit C. It was furnished – or as the law calls it, "published" – to the jury. The women jurors studied each page and photograph, but the men did not have the stomach for it and passed the exhibit on after a quick look, as if it were poison. All twelve members looked drawn and pale. Three of the women hung their heads.

I passed the witness to O'Bannon, who didn't bother to rise. He said, "Nothing, Your Honor."

I had intended calling Sam's friends at this point on the issue of his bragging about his abuse of Betty. I conferred with Drew quickly. He agreed we didn't need to risk it. They might try to inject something we didn't want, along with what we were interested in.

I had the momentum now, and I didn't want to change anything. The same thinking applied to the reputation witnesses we had lined up. Betty's testimony regarding Sam's use of the shotgun barrel had been supported with solid evidence, and I didn't think the jury needed corroboration of her truthfulness.

One material question still remained. Why didn't Betty leave when she had the chance?

CHAPTER 34

Defense Calls Jim Drew and Dr. Rob Willoby

By day four of any trial, every trial lawyer knows the jury has filled out its scorecard, made out its batting order, and nearly decided the final score. The issues are well established, and the lawyer's proclivities are likewise – which lawyer is delivering the facts, and which one is trying to kick dirt.

That morning, I hoped I was seeing things clearly as I set my briefcase on the table in the courtroom. I figured it was time to make sure every question counted and move to the end before the jury got sick of it all and quit listening.

I started the day with Jim Drew. His investigation would

remind the jury why we were there – the bloody mistake of the gun going off. And then those intriguing side issues he spotted. The frosting on the cake.

Drew knew the ropes. He'd been on the stand numerous times during his MSP service. We went through his credentials and emphasized his police background and training. He was a straightforward professional.

He testified he'd run down the ownership of the blue Chevy with the license plate beginning with HBV that we'd seen pull up to Betty's home on the day of the incident.

"The owner is Elsa Howard, address 1743 Knollwood," he said. "I got the registration from the Secretary of State's office and went to her home. The car was there, the key was in the ignition, and I noticed a receipt lying on the back seat in plain view. I took a photo of it through the window, and when I enlarged it, it was a Wick's receipt for a roll of plastic sheeting."

He held up a photo. He'd got the photo without trespassing.

He continued, and tied the evidence to Sam Waterman's mistress. "I went to Wick's and found the clerk who'd sold the plastic. She recalled the transaction, and, when I showed her a picture of six similar women, she picked out Elsa as the woman who purchased it."

O'Bannon glumly declined to cross-examine. It was plain he wasn't sure how to act, so he took the safe course by not acting. I intended to go fast with my proofs before he got back in the fight.

I next called Dr. Rob Willoby and led him through his qualifications in psychology. I drew out his methodology and then went right to the point: He had done a psychological exam of Betty and Beth shortly after the shooting. His report was offered to the prosecution and as Defense Exhibit D.

"How many pages is your report?" I asked him.

"Fourteen," he answered.

"For full disclosure to the jury, are you being paid for

your testimony here today?"

He smiled and shook his head. "Well, I'm not paid for my testimony. I'm paid for my professional time to attend this trial. I am charging much less than my normal fees to cover costs. I have testified for the prosecution and for the defense in a number of trials and have never charged my regular fees for those services. I believe it is my duty as a professional psychologist to offer my expertise in criminal cases involving emotional trauma. I am being paid the customary fee I charge all patients for additional therapy sessions."

I opened the gate and invited him to run as far as he could.

"Dr. Willoby, you have authored a report with your conclusions, correct?"

I led him through the foundation required to admit the report, then asked if it could be admitted officially in evidence. O'Bannon waved me off when I put it in front of him, as if it had no relevance.

"Any objection to its admission?" Judge Blevin asked.

"Nope," he replied. Bad answer. The right answer is to stand anytime you address the court and make your comment respectfully, such as, "No, Your Honor."

Blevin arched an eyebrow at O'Bannon, and said, "I'm sorry, counsel, I didn't hear your response to my question."

O'Bannon heard the roll of distant thunder in the judge's voice and snapped to attention so quickly that even the jury understood the breach of etiquette. He rose from his chair and said, "No objection, Your Honor."

Two jurors smirked at him.

Nothing feels better than your opponent putting himself in the doghouse, especially when your expert witness might face some skepticism.

It's almost axiomatic in jury trials that a jury goes in the direction signaled by the judge, and this judge was not buying Jerry O'Bannon's rudeness and disrespect for the system.

I motioned for Willoby to continue. "Go on," I said.

He picked up easily, "As I started to say, the report is fourteen pages. The first few pages are the summary – a history – of what Betty told me. Then there's some standard tests, like the MMPI."

We had discussed all this, and this was one issue I wanted to make sure would stick in the jury's mind. I said, "Can you tell the jury the purpose of the MMPI?"

He turned to the jury and held up the document. "On page seven of the report, there is an explanation of the test and the result. MMPI stands for 'Minnesota Multi-Phasic Inventory.' It's a psychological test protocol developed in the late 1930s and includes a standardized measure for malingering, dissembling – what we commonly think of as lying. It's used almost universally by professionals who do psychological assessments."

"Really?" I said with feigned ignorance. I had used the test many times with previous clients. It was a way to address the core issue of any trial – truthfulness of a defendant without asking a blatantly self-serving question.

"Yes," he answered. "It's a test with some tricks in it to catch a person who is not putting forth their best effort or is making false claims."

I prompted him. "And to a reasonable degree of scientific certainty, what did Betty's test results establish?"

"The test results were negative," he said.

"Is that good or bad?" I asked, to make sure the jury understood that "negative" did not mean "bad."

"'Negative' means there was no evidence of lying. If the test were 'positive,' it would signal a red flag that something was wrong. In this test, Mrs. Waterman gave her best effort. In other words, she was telling the truth," he said.

"As part of the history she gave you, did she explain what happened in this incident?" I asked.

The jury was right with him, listening intently.

"Yes, she did," he answered. "She told me the same history she told the police. She picked up the shotgun for fear

Waterman would use it on her. She had a sudden vision of Waterman putting her little girl, Beth, into the furnace. Then she heard an overwhelming sound inside of her head, and the next thing she knew the gun went off. She hadn't seen anything, she hadn't done anything, and her husband was a bloody mess on the bed."

"And the test results indicated she was telling the truth," I stated. In truth, it was a blatant leading question that O'Bannon pretended to ignore. If he objected, he just would have drawn attention to the answer.

"Thank you, doctor," I said. I liked repeating the word 'doctor' as much as possible, because a jury instinctively respects doctors. "You may go ahead with your testimony regarding your examination and therapy."

"Mrs. Waterman and I have spoken at length about that morning and her psychological condition at that time as well as during the three plus years of her marriage to Sam Waterman," he said. "I believe in her mind, and perhaps, in fact, Waterman was about to kill her and Beth. What happened was the product of genuine fear and certainty of his intent."

"When you refer to 'what happened,' what are you referring to?" I asked.

"The gun going off." He looked at the jury now. "She didn't intend it, and isn't sure why it happened."

"What do you think happened?" I asked, knowing what his answer would be.

He turned to Judge Blevin as he answered, "That is the jury's role, isn't it?" And the judge nodded in agreement.

We were all headed in the same direction—the judge, the witness, me. And we were all making the jury feel we trusted them, so they could rely on us for the truth. But this little colloquy was one I planned so the subject we were discussing would stand out in the jury's mind.

"I agree," I said, "that's the jury's role. Let me rephrase the question. Based on what Betty described and what her test results show, can you tell the jury what you concluded about her state of mind?"

"At the time of the incident?" he asked. As we had planned. I indicated yes.

"We don't know why the shotgun went off, but I can say to a reasonable degree of scientific certainty that at the moment it went off, Mrs. Waterman was out of her mind. She was envisioning a horrible death for her little girl. There was a dissociative urge. She heard an overwhelming sound in her head, and she was not aware of where she was or what was happening."

He held up his palms in surrender to what he knew.

"Do you mean she suffers from mental illness?" I asked.

"No, she does not. She does not suffer from dissociative identity syndrome, or what a lay person would call a split personality." He paused, to let that sink in. "But in that moment, there was a dissociative impact on her of the abuse, the dead kitten, the threats, and the vision of her daughter being burned to death. She was unable to think, plan, or control her actions."

He waited for me to ask the next question.

"Although you cannot say exactly what happened, are you able to say whether Betty's mental state – her dissociative moment – is a reliable fact in this case?"

He looked at me, then the jury. "I can say to a scientific certainty it was. She was in a state of mind that is a recognized fact in the field of psychology, and has been studied and treated." He stopped.

"Have you treated her?" I asked.

"No, not for that illness. The testing I did indicated she does not suffer from the ongoing illness. Her working diagnosis is related to PTSD, the damage of long-term abuse and stress."

I motioned for him to continue.

"Betty had a moment that was similar in kind, but different in duration to dissociative syndrome. It was what we refer to as a transitory dissociation. It was situational."

I asked, "Is she a risk to herself or society?"

"No," he said quickly and surely. "The only risk is that Betty will carry a sense of guilt that makes her a risk for future depression."

"Is that what you're treating her for at this time?" I asked.

"Exactly," he answered. "The persistent, continuous abuse she endured was on a scale beyond anything I have ever seen or heard and has caused nightmares for me, despite my long-term exposure to what I would call normal abuse.

"The horror of that abuse, coupled with Waterman's credible threat of death, constituted an imminent danger in her mind and caused her to dissociate in that moment. It's like someone says they blacked out. Well, in this case she blacked out, in a manner of speaking, because her brain would not accept or process the scream in her head and the vision of her child being burned to death."

He paused for a moment. "It is my opinion that, whatever happened, she could not have stopped Sam's death."

"Does she have remorse over what happened?" I asked.

"That is the most difficult part of this. I'm sure it's why she told the police she must be guilty. Even though she doesn't know what happened, the sight of him dead and the gun in her hands – well, she's a Quaker and has a very strong sense of guilt for having been involved in any way."

I played the last card I had with Willoby. "You mentioned you also tested Beth, her three-year-old," I said.

He nodded. "I did not do any paper tests, like the MMPI, because obviously you can't do that with a toddler. Pediatric neuron-psychological testing is only vaguely possible."

"Was there anything reliable you were able to do?" I asked, and waited for the answer he'd given me during our prep.

"I can say this with the requisite scientific reliability. When I questioned her, it was obvious that little girl knows something happened, but as every parent on the jury knows," he started, and then he paused and scanned the jurors' faces, "the limitation is that she is not able to formulate the words to express what she saw and the impact it had on her."

The effect was to meld the jury to his next statement. "When you question a child of that age forensically, it's critically important not to offer suggestions. So, I asked Beth an open-ended question – 'Did you see someone hurt?'

"She said she did, by nodding. She repeated 'hurt,'" Willoby paused again.

O'Bannon objected quickly. "Judge, this is rank hearsay."

I was just as quick to respond. "Your Honor, this is a well-recognized exception to hearsay under Michigan Rule of Evidence 803(4). It's a statement made in response to an open-ended question in the course of a treatment session."

Blevin looked at O'Bannon with an arched eyebrow. I couldn't tell if he was daring him, or genuinely considering his objection.

Blevin finally said, "I'm looking at you, Mr. O'Bannon, to see whether you have a response to Mr. Nichols's reference to the rule of evidence."

O'Bannon looked unsure of himself. A blusterer by nature, he had only a passing familiarity with legal research. I'd prepared to handle the possibility of an objection before I ever asked the question.

"I don't think it needs a response," O'Bannon replied.

Judge Blevin cast a wearied eye that was close to rolling his eyes. He said with more tact than deserved, "Well, counsel, hearing no further argument, I am going to exercise my discretion to admit the statement made in response to an open-ended question during therapy."

"May I continue with this line of questioning, Your Honor?" I asked, wanting to be sure of my footing before eliciting another statement.

Judge Blevin nodded. "I am going to ask you to respect the fact we are in territory that has some legal significance. Other than that, you may proceed."

"Dr. Willoby, did she make any other statement during

your therapy?" I asked.

He said, "I asked, 'Who was hurt?' and she said, 'Sam hurt Mommy, Mommy crying.'" Suddenly Willoby looked away from the jury, and his eyes filled.

It must have been the accumulated stress of the trial, the subject, the abject sadness of the entire case. I had not been prepared for emotion from an expert witness. The jury saw what was happening before their eyes. It almost affected me.

"From the mouths of babes," Willoby quoted the old saying.

The women wiped their eyes and the men sat uncomfortably as though at attention. The jury was in subtle motion like wind-driven prairie grass, jurors shifting in their seats, pulling handkerchiefs, leaning forward to look directly at Betty, sitting alone at the table, as tears ran down her face.

"The defense rests," I said.

O'Bannon didn't dare question Willoby.

I asked Blevin for a ten-minute recess, and he nodded to the bailiff and jury. "Ten minutes it is."

....

I had just received a note that Stella had called, and I reached her immediately. Lewis Castle had fired me as his attorney in his accident case and picked up his files. It was a case I'd counted on for a hefty contingency fee, and the loss of it drove home the risk to my practice for taking on Betty's cause. Midway through trial, there was nothing I could do about it.

I breathed into the phone as my mind raced. Stella was waiting for some kind of reaction. "Stella, tell him I love him no matter what, and I am fighting for an abused woman's life."

I couldn't think of anything more. Stella said wearily, "You're a good guy, Robert." It sounded halfway between praise and an indictment.

Somehow, I suddenly felt vulnerable, sitting at the counsel table, the survival of my practice at stake, but without the time or energy to do anything about it. It felt as if I was out of sync with everything. Moving in slow motion.

I willed myself to get my focus back. In the middle of a trial, nothing else matters. It can't. It's in motion, and it is the peak of the meaning of the profession of law. It's like a runner being given bad news in the middle of a race.

I did what trial lawyers do and sometimes regret mightily. I wiped every concern from my mind except Betty's defense.

We had momentum. I had the jury's complete attention during the morning. I had the jurors' tears. I had O'Bannon on the ropes. I had the truth.

Both Drew and Willoby had scored unanswered points. I was sure most of the jurors believed Betty and were moving in her direction, but I couldn't tell if her case would stick until the end.

The die – at least my die – was cast. When I announced I would rest the case that was that. I would sit and see what O'Bannon had hidden up his sleeve, if anything.

Law practice? What law practice?

I knew one sure thing. O'Bannon's rebuttal witness, Arti Brown, would be crucial. We had bet on truth as our defense, and he would try to tear the truth apart. My cross-examination would be the linchpin of the case. There was no place for me to hide.

Self-doubt was there, gnawing on me. It was the burden of my feelings for Betty. And Betty sensed it. She squeezed my hand, staring straight ahead with a smile. She was a knockout, and I almost flushed.

Arti Brown, the prosecution's psychiatrist, boasted a record of convictions that was remarkable in our county. He was a professional witness, whose spark and spackle could easily fool a jury.

I thought it was more likely he would fall into the same trap as Jerry, believing the case was a slam dunk. Instead of doing genuine research and study, he'd depend on his resume and expensive suit to get by.

One thing I had going for me: Brown was so well known and his standard dodges so obvious, that I felt sure I knew what he'd say and how he'd say it. That and a bit of surprise research.

CHAPTER 35

Prosecution, Rebuttal, Dr. Arti Brown

Judge Blevin resumed his chair on the bench, squared himself, and directed his attention to O'Bannon.

"Does the prosecution wish to call any rebuttal, Mr. O'Bannon?" he asked.

O'Bannon rose and swaggered to the podium. It was the first swagger in more than a day, and I was sure it was feigned. But with a truly gifted swaggerer, you can never be certain.

"Dr. Artemeus Brown, MD," he announced more loudly than necessary. Doubling the witness's credentials – Dr. and MD – was the epitome of his style.

Dr. Brown was a professional witness and used to relying on his resume and presentation in place of genuine research or study. With some luck on that end and the terrific research Jim had done on his trial records, I thought we had a real chance to tear him a new asshole. Having considered him a sanctimonious son of a bitch, I was hoping my expectation he would fail to prepare proved right. We needed his shortcomings to be on full display as the last piece of our defense puzzle.

Brown approached the court clerk for the oath. As he raised his hand to be sworn, he looked over his shoulder at the jury with an abnormally bright smile. He sported a British-type tweed jacket, sharply creased slacks and a cravat. He had an elegant cane in his left hand.

Seating himself in the witness box, he leaned back in the chair and smiled again at the jury, flashing his brilliantly white, straight teeth. I thought my two best jurors rolled their eyes slightly.

"Will you tell us your name and occupation, Dr. Brown?" Jerry asked.

He replied that he'd been a practicing psychiatrist in this town for twenty-two years, with an office in the Citizens Bank building.

O'Bannon elicited Brown's credentials, which Brown crisply recited. It took several minutes. He knew every comma and hyphen of his resume by heart. It was common for lawyers like O'Bannon to select experts based on their resume, rather than their honesty. O'Bannon was counting on Brown, the psychiatrist with a medical degree, to outshine Rob Willoby, a genuine, practicing psychologist.

"Dr. Brown," he started questioning in a stage voice, "Have you examined Mrs. Waterman, the defendant?"

"Yes, I have," he responded in an equally inflated stage voice, as if it were a meaningful accomplishment. He and O'Bannon had performed this act many times.

Brown was seated somewhat sideways, facing the jury, poised to shower them with his full attention. It was sort of what I'd counseled my own witnesses to do. A witness has to be reminded to speak to the jury when appropriate. But this version of that was too mannered, like vaudeville. A witness who doesn't face the examining lawyer is obviously a trained seal. You wait for him to open his mouth for a treat.

"Have you formed an opinion regarding her truthfulness in her description of the circumstances surrounding her shooting of her husband, Sam Waterman?" O'Bannon was getting right down to business.

"Yes, I have. And no, Mrs. Waterman was most certainly not telling the truth," Dr. Brown said, his voice filling the room.

He hadn't posed his answer in acceptable terms, legally. I started for an instant to object, but kept still instead. He was a trained seal after all. I'd bide my time until I had the harpoon sharpened. Objecting to mere opinion dulls the cutting edge.

"And your conclusions are based on ...?" O'Bannon went on.

"Well, sir, I asked her to tell me her complete story," he said, "including her years of marriage with the deceased, Sam Waterman. She told me about her education at Michigan State University and her grief at the loss of her best friend to cancer. She admitted her liaison with Sam had come about as the result of drinking too much at a bar while grieving her friend's death. She claimed, without any evidence to support it, that she was drugged and raped by Sam and later discovered she was pregnant. She only married Sam for convenience. She confided that she planned to get a divorce when it suited her. Frankly, her whole presentation was quite opportunistic. I would say narcissistic.

"In my professional opinion, her statements about the alleged abuse she suffered were fanciful and overblown. The abuse she alleged was so extreme, it defied belief. Let me say this: If she had been telling the truth, why did she not leave him long ago?" He raised his eyebrows theatrically at the jury.

"It seemed obvious her real complaint was her husband's demand for wifely performance in the bedroom. Such a complaint flies in the face of Michigan law and custom. My conclusion is that she duped the decedent into a marriage of convenience, killed him for reasons known only to herself, and is lying simply to enhance her defense."

He stopped and wiped his lips with his pocket handkerchief.

It was a performance, pure and simple. I studied the jury for their reaction.

The phrase 'wifely performance' had clearly struck a nerve in several of the women jurors, who now looked at Brown as if he had stepped in something foul on the way to court.

O'Bannon was too focused on his notes to notice the jury's reaction to Brown. He barged ahead.

"In fact, what is Michigan's law and custom as it relates to Betty's complaints of marital rape?" he asked.

I was on my feet before the question mark at the end of the sentence was out of his mouth.

"Your Honor, I object. The question concerning Michigan law is beyond this witness's professional expertise. That question can only be answered by a judge," I said, and sat down so the jury's sole focus would be on Judge Blevin and O'Bannon. It was a valid, no-brainer objection.

O'Bannon's personality was preloaded. There was an easy way out of my objection, but he didn't go there. As usual, he opted for the pugnacity of his elected office.

"Judge Blevin," he began with a sniff and exaggerated eye roll, "the defense knows perfectly well what I was asking. The defense knows when I ..."

Blevin cut him off. "Your response to the objection, Mr. O'Bannon, is precisely what?" He locked his eyes on the prosecutor and held the stare.

"Dr. Brown is an expert, and he has testified numerous times and he knows exactly what the law is, in such cases."

O'Bannon was so sure of himself, he looked at the jury, and I thought I saw him wink.

"Counsel," Blevin started, "I do not know how many times this witness has testified," and he gestured at Brown without looking, "but I am sustaining the objection. Mr. Brown is not an authority on Michigan law, to my knowledge. He may testify to his field of psychiatry, but he may not testify about Michigan law – or any other law – until he gets his law degree and runs for my job."

It was a bit of humor for the jury, and they got it. They gave a short burst of laughter. From the look on O'Bannon's face, it was apparent he felt the knife slip between his ribs.

Brown had turned away from the jury and was looking at O'Bannon for guidance, and O'Bannon clearly was looking for a segue to his notes. A single drop of sweat ran down the hairline next to his left ear.

It would be the height of arrogance to claim I see everything in a courtroom, but it's no overstatement to say I try to see everything. I try to filter every atom in the courtroom through my brain. The core task of trial work is processing every possible input to the jury and processing every possible output from the jury.

That may seem to be at odds with my professed belief in truth and justice, but I take it as my duty of due care. In the close confines of a courtroom, there are influences, and they are fluid. The hope is to stay with a good flow and redirect a bad flow. For that, you need to know the flow.

This time, I felt it. The flow.

O'Bannon was ruffled, his witness was unsure, and the jury's accusatory attention on O'Bannon was palpable.

O'Bannon had failed to prep Brown for the facts, instead relying on his chosen theme – the marital rape mantra. Now with Judge Blevin nixing his plan for the witness, he was at a loss of where to turn.

O'Bannon tried to start over, and the first words out of his mouth told me where he was headed.

"In your professional experience, have you evaluated other women making the same sort of allegations that Mrs. Waterman is making about her husband?"

"Her complaints," Brown said, picking up the relay baton, "were exactly the same complaints many wives make. As you know, the marital rape exception does not deem the physical assault of one's wife for sexual services a crime. Betty knew she was required to freely give sexual service to her husband but was unwilling to act within the law of marital exception."

I stood. I did not rush, because Brown and O'Bannon were frozen by my presence, and I wanted to prolong the moment. An old mentor had once said, if you have a killer point, give it a little drum roll.

"Judge Blevin, the term 'marital exception' is a legal term. When I objected before, I believe I heard you indicate the parameters of this witness's permissible testimony. He just violated your order."

I sat down to luxuriate as Judge Blevin scowled, which was as focused on O'Bannon as a cat's attention is on a bird next to the feeder.

I barely moved my hand to place it on Betty's arm. Underneath the cloth of her dress I sensed her skin and felt something more than warmth, and heard her exhale softly. It was a moment of intimacy that was sensual and secret. She had sensed the same thing in the moment as I.

"Mr. O'Bannon, your response to the objection," Judge Blevin clasped his hands in prayer fashion against his pursed lips.

O'Bannon tried to duck, the cowardly way, by blaming the witness. "I didn't intend to elicit that answer, Your Honor."

"Are you saying you didn't prepare this witness to testify about some legal concept?" Blevin pressed.

"Uh, I'm not exactly saying that, Your Honor," he stammered.

"Mr. O'Bannon, if you are unsure exactly what to say, I will now give the jury a curative instruction that will help you with what to say." Judge Blevin was a fair judge, and what he was about to do would be fair. But it would be harsh, as every curative instruction is.

A curative instruction is what a judge does when he

or she feels an attorney or a witness has done something wrong – usually intentionally wrong – to bias the trial. The judge has to set things right, and the only way to do it is to tell the jury something that would change what had just happened.

It was never good to be on the receiving end, because a curative instruction cut through a lot of vagary and outright nonsense in no uncertain terms.

"Mr. Brown, I want you to listen to this carefully," Judge Blevin said, clearing his throat before going on. "Ladies and gentlemen of the jury, I am going to sustain the defense's objection to the witness's use of the phrase 'marital exception.' It is, as the defense objected, a legal term. It is an old, almost antique phrase signifying a certain benighted element of our legal system."

As the judge paused to gather his thoughts before going on, I squeezed Betty's arm, and I could feel her breath as if it were my own, but I couldn't return her look for fear I would publicly expose my feelings.

"It is not a phrase you will hear again from this witness. Am I right, Dr. Brown?" and Brown nodded his head so quickly and enthusiastically, it would have been comedic if the room had not been so charged with tension.

My two jurors, as I had come to think of them, almost laughed aloud.

"The reason you will not hear it again is the same reason the phrase 'marital exception' and 'rape immunity' and 'wifely duties' will almost certainly someday disappear from the courtrooms of Michigan, and from the vocabulary of the community." He seemed to be breathing hard through his nostrils between sentences. "As a judge, I am bound by the rules of antiquity. I might add that a jury has its own rules. A jury must follow the rules as instructed by the court, but then the jury must also apply its own common sense and experience.

"You have both duties – duty to the law and duty to common sense and experience. I am sure all of you understand what I am saying. I would like each of you, as I call your number, to indicate by a nod of your head that you understand your duty to follow the law and your concomitant duty to apply your own common sense and experience to the facts of this case."

Blevin stopped and went down the line of jurors. "Juror #1, do you understand?" He went number by number. They all nodded.

I thought I had the two of them, but there were seven jurors who, when it came their turn to nod, didn't just nod "yes." They nodded "hell yes."

"Okay, Mr. O'Bannon, you may continue. I think we are all aware of our responsibility now."

I felt something had changed. Every person in that courtroom had just heard the ponderous door of history creak open on the issue of the marital rape exception. Judge Blevin had just administered the healthy oil of common sense to the hinges.

O'Bannon had heard the same turning of the gears of history. The judge had just invited the jury to listen to the instructions he would give them, but then to use their common sense to ignore those instructions.

He effectively said: "The law said a husband could rape and abuse his wife at will. But really, are you going to follow that law?"

The concept of jury nullification is a seldom discussed rule in the law school or the courts. The courts' primary role is to enforce the law as it exists. Judge Blevin had just made jury nullification the controlling feature of the case.

O'Bannon, like every lawyer who has been crushed by an adverse ruling, just wanted to figure out a way to get back to his seat without further embarrassment. He made one last attempt.

"As you know, irresistible impulse requires direct, illegal confrontation. Yet Sam Waterman, the deceased, engaged in no illegal action prior to being murdered. How could he? He was sound asleep! This defense is not viable, but simply a desperate attempt to excuse the defendant's inde-fensible actions."

It was not remotely a question. We all knew it. O'Bannon waited for Brown's answer. I stood to object.

"Objection, lead–," I said,

Judge Blevin said, "Sustained," before I could finish. He was not the sort of judge who smacked a gavel. He was the sort whose look of frustration at the offended counsel conveyed more than any gavel could.

O'Bannon's sweat was running freely, and Brown looked like a deer in the headlights.

"Pass the witness," O'Bannon said as he slunk back to his chair.

Then he stopped, and turned. "Wait, I forgot to ask for the admission of this expert's report. I move to admit the report," he finished lamely.

I objected on grounds the report contained a refer-ence to the "marital exception." "Your Honor," I started to explain, but Blevin interrupted politely.

He said, "Counsel, I agree with you that the reference to that phrase must be stricken. But you know as well as I that if I throw out the baby with the bathwater, it might open the door to an appeals court to throw out the whole trial."

He waited for my response. He was right. With the trial going my way, I didn't want a juicy appeal issue.

"I understand, Your Honor," I said. "I will withdraw my objection to the report with the understanding the offend-ing phrase will be redacted."

"Thank you, counsel, that's a wise choice," Blevin said. He looked at O'Bannon and added, "You understand what that means, Mr. O'Bannon? Careful redaction?"

O'Bannon quickly said, "Yes, thank you, Your Honor."

Arti Brown's head had been going back and forth between me, O'Bannon and the judge, like a tennis specta-tor. Now I focused on him. I luxuriated in the fearful look on his face as I organized my notes. I'd read the report, and it was scurrilous. Brown had gone overboard writing his criticisms and defamations of Betty's character.

That was back when he thought he was writing about a slam-dunk guilty person. Things had changed. Brown had been humbled by Judge Blevin's rulings and by O'Bannon's lack of preparation. And Betty had been elevated by the trial testimony.

There was no more slam dunk. And his report's overboard comments no longer would seem fair to the jury.

Normally, I do not have the heart to destroy a witness who has already been destroyed. What goes around comes around. I just don't tempt the fates by piling on. Normally.

But nothing was normal. I was hopelessly linked to Betty now, and my personal feelings for her cried out to me to vindicate her.

I couldn't resist. I had prepared a cross-examination that was strong. In the aftermath of Judge Blevin's rulings that limited Brown's permissible testimony, my exam would be even stronger.

CHAPTER 36

Defense Cross of Dr. Brown

I cleared my throat, licked my finger, inhaled, and as I looked up, I smiled at Brown to let him know I was going to enjoy filleting him.

I was going to force Brown to walk through a minefield. One more misstep by him in violation of Blevin's curative instruction could lead to disaster for him. If he violated the rule one more time, a contempt ruling by Blevin was likely, and it would haunt him in every case for the rest of his career: "Aren't you the same Dr. Arti Brown who was held in contempt in this court on a previous occasion when you intentionally violated the rules established by the trial judge?"

He eyed me, and I could almost visualize the leash around his neck. I picked up my end of the leash.

"Dr. Brown, good morning," I said. "Are you appearing as an expert in this case?"

He assented tersely, "Yes."

I went on. "When Mr. O'Bannon hired you to testify, you knew nothing about Betty Waterman."

He couldn't resist the urge to fight. "Well, I also knew what I'd read in the newspaper and heard on the evening news."

"And what you'd read and heard provided you additional basis for your expert opinions?" I asked innocently.

"Of course, everything does ..." he started and then I saw his eyes shift from me to something behind me. I realized he'd just gotten a signal from O'Bannon, who had spotted the trap I'd just set.

"Everything does," I repeated for the record. "You just said that, correct?"

Brown knew something was wrong with his answer, based on O'Bannon's signal. The problem was, Brown didn't know what was wrong. All he knew was his answer was wrong.

"Well, I didn't say exactly that," his voice clearly sounded guarded.

I asked the court reporter to read back Brown's last answer. It was exactly what I'd heard, and exactly what I'd asked, and exactly what Brown had just denied.

"You did, indeed say, 'Everything does,' in response to my question," I said with a tone of accusation. It was a pointed start to a cross-exam of an expert, and I was going to drive the point right through him.

"Well, I suppose I did," he admitted.

"And you know, under the Michigan rules of evidence, an expert, such as yourself," and here I added a dash of tone – not an objectionable dash, but a discernible dash – of sarcasm, "has to disclose all the bases for his opinions."

Now he knew where I was going, and it was too late. "Yes," he said simply.

"And you relied, in part, on information you got from the news, isn't that right?" I continued.

Arti Brown, MD, expert psychiatrist for the prosecution, sensed he was in trouble. A courtroom silence somehow sounds louder than the actual sound.

There was silence. O'Bannon couldn't object. Brown

slowly answered as he had to, "Yes, I suppose I partly relied on that information."

"So, you relied on hearsay, what a news reporter said?" I asked, driving the point deeper.

"Yes, partly," he said, his face flushing now.

I looked at the jury and gave a small nod, as if disgusted.

"That's what we call rank speculation, isn't it?" I asked, still looking at the jury. They were ready to enjoy the demise of this witness.

Every witness had a finite limit of tolerance, after which they become combative, just because combat is the last line of defense. That was the line I had hoped to evoke. I wanted Arti Brown, MD, to be combative, because that would provide me cover when I really went on the attack.

An attorney who attacks a witness without justification risks the jury's ire. Attorneys are, after all, as everyone knows, cheats and opportunists. I knew I had to be fair and square – I couldn't be the first one to throw a punch. So, I threw him the "speculation" issue in the hope he would attack me.

He attacked. "My so-called speculation is solidly based with my extensive training – I would be happy to review my curriculum vitae again for you, if you didn't understand it the first time."

"I have that and I have your report," I said.

"Perhaps you should have read it more carefully before you came to court this morning," he said archly.

"What about relying on news reporters for your opinions?" I said. "Isn't it true you did that?"

"You know perfectly well that I said 'partly,'" he said.

"So, your opinion is speculation, partly," I said, not really a question, but a statement that demanded an answer.

He shook his head as if unable to make sense to me. "My dear man, my report is anything but speculation. It is factual and true and based on my expert training."

"So, except for disclosing your reliance on the news – in part," I added to make sure he would go for the bait, "everything in the report is true?"

And he bit hard. "Absolutely, and you of all people should know that based on my reputation as an expert," he said, crossing his arms as if to close the subject.

I smiled falsely. "Dr. Brown, I confess I am less experienced than you are, but I know a lie when I hear one."

There was a silently clanging bell in the courtroom. There was no bell but there was a silence like a bell would make if bells could ring silently.

"Dr. Brown," I said, "this brings me to a certified copy of the Genesee County Jail records for October 20, the date you testified you met with Betty at her jail cell."

I held up the document and moved for its admission as Defense Exhibit E.

O'Bannon started to rise, but Judge Blevin waved him to sit down.

"Mr. O'Bannon, do you have an objection to this authentic official business record?" the judge asked.

Blevin, without saying anything specific, adroitly cited three rules of evidence that would allow the admission of the document. O'Bannon prudently sat down and avoided the embarrassment of objecting and being denied once again.

"The document is admitted as E," Blevin said without looking up again.

I approached the witness box and handed Brown the document.

"Before I question you about this exhibit, I have a preliminary question for you: How much have you been paid to so obviously and dramatically commit perjury before these jurors?"

This time there was an audible gasp from the jurors, and they leaned forward in their chairs. It was a belligerent, lawyerly question, and for that reason it is rarely asked. But I'd laid the foundation for it carefully, and I knew the jury would tolerate it.

Brown straightened up in the witness chair and actually

shook his fist at me.

"This is absurd and deeply insulting. I have told the complete truth to this jury, and you do not have the competence or ethical standards required to make such an incredible charge. I demand that you retract your scurrilous accusation." He sniffed loudly for emphasis.

My "nice" act was over. He'd bit, gone on the attack, and now anything I did was fair.

"The 'complete truth' you say?" I repeated it to emphasize his statement. "Dr. Brown, I would willingly retract my statement if I could. Unfortunately, I cannot, because what I said is accurate. Will you answer my question?"

"As for the first part of your question, I'm paid $600 per hour for courtroom testimony," he said. "As for the second part of your question, I have committed no perjury. The report is true."

"Your report says you performed – and I quote – 'an extensive two-hour clinical interview' of Betty at the Genesee County Jail. Is that correct?" I showed him the page of his report. He didn't look.

"That is what it says," he answered.

"And you know Betty testified you spent less than ten minutes with her, correct?" I asked.

"I am aware she claims that," he said.

"I want you to look at this exhibit, sir," I said, handing him a one-page document.

He took it, glanced at it. Now he knew what I was doing. The corner of his right eye started to twitch.

"Will you tell the jury what that document is, sir?" I asked.

"It appears to be the jail visitor log from October," he said. His voice had weakened suddenly.

"And did it record your visit to Betty?" I asked.

"That is what it says," he replied. There was sweat shining on his forehead.

"And how long does the official jail log say you were there?" I asked. Instead of answering me, he pretended to be reading. Just eight lines on the page, but he read and read.

I looked at the jury, letting the silence deepen. It seemed clear enough that Arti Brown would never be able to finish reading the eight lines by the end of the trial.

I shook my head slightly and said, "According to this official record, Defense Exhibit E, it is true, is it not, just as Betty said, you were with her less than ten minutes on the twentieth of October? Or do you dispute this official record?"

Brown took a deep breath, wiping away the sweat glistening on his brow.

"Apparently, it is correct," he stammered. "I apologize for the lapse of memory."

"Dr. Brown," I said, now aiming for the coup de grace. "Mr. O'Bannon submitted your report in evidence, and you stated under oath that your report was true and accurate. Am I recalling that correctly?"

He nodded. I prompted him, "I need an audible answer so the court reporter can make a record."

He responded, "Yes."

"But your report is not truthful, is it?" I prodded him. "And Betty's statement was true, wasn't it?"

"Yes," he said.

"Which question did you just answer?" I said, toying with him. "The one about your report not being truthful or the one about Betty's statement being true?"

"The answer to both is the same answer," he croaked.

"Then may I have your full answer?" I asked. You want an answer like this one to sing in the courtroom.

"Yes, my report is not truthful, and yes, Betty's statement was true."

Now that I had jerked the leash hard enough to make sure Arti Brown, MD, would heel nicely, I went to the substance of my cross-exam.

"You have already testified to this jury that she told you her complete story, about how she came to marry Sam

Waterman and years of ugly abuse, have you not?"

Sweat trickled down his face, and the veins were visible on his neck.

"Yes," he said.

"In fact, Dr. Brown, you really only had enough time to ask her to confirm her name and age and that she was the defendant in the case after introducing yourself and explaining why you were there, is that not true?"

He squeezed out a fearful, compliant, "Yes."

"In fact, you have never heard the defendant talk about her background story at any time and never made notes of that meeting, is that not true?" I asked.

Brown stared ahead, red-faced, at a nonexistent spot in the courtroom, avoiding the jury's gaze.

"Yes," he said, his voice a whisper. He was staring at O'Bannon for help, an objection, anything, but O'Bannon would not raise his eyes from his notepad. The sweat was running full tide now, and Brown brushed away at it with a crisp, white handkerchief.

"Did you or did you not get all your facts from the prosecutor?" I could feel the point of my questioning hit the heart muscle of O'Bannon's case.

"Yes," he mumbled.

"It was hard to hear you," I said. "Did you just answer yes – you got all your facts in this case from the prosecutor?"

I looked at the jury with the smallest hint of well-earned satisfaction.

Brown looked away from me and the jury but said the only thing he could say, "Yes," this time louder. "She did not make those statements directly to me."

"As an expert, do you often rely on a layperson, such as the prosecuting attorney in this case, to do clinical interviews for you?"

"No," he answered as his spirit left his body, and he gave up any pretense of defending his report.

There is a point when a courtroom collectively reaches finality about a witness – whether credible or incredible – and that point had passed for Arti Brown, MD. And he knew it.

He'd made a mistake, and he was sorry. That's all he had left.

"Since you now admit she told you nothing that could even be compared with her statement to the prosecutor, you must now admit it is impossible for you, personally, to have made a sound judgment as to her truthfulness, isn't that correct, doctor?"

"Yes," he said softly.

His face was bright red from the stress, like a man who had run a mile, and I let him sit there and sweat for what seemed much longer, but in reality, was only seconds of silence. I then asked him for an audible answer again. He hung his head and looked up at the judge as though in prayer for deliverance.

"Yes," he said too loudly.

"And you cannot make any criticism of Betty's truthfulness, correct?" I stated and waited.

"Correct," he said too loudly, to avoid having to do it twice. My leash had him at heel.

"Though your report calls Betty a liar, you don't really have a basis for that opinion, correct?" I asked.

"Correct," he said loudly.

"But you wrote that she lied, didn't you?" I asked.

"I said it was based on my long experience as a trained psychiatrist," he said.

"I asked you, Dr. Brown, what it was she said that told you so immediately she was a liar."

"It was not what she said but how she said it," he answered.

"What does that mean?" I asked.

"She was far too composed and responded too easily to my questions without the hesitation normal for an accused murderer," he said.

"Your Honor, I ask you to strike Dr. Brown's testimony calling Betty Waterman, who sits before the jury an innocent woman, an accused murderer." I had an edge of controlled outrage in my voice.

Judge Blevin made short work of the good doctor.

"The statement is hereby struck from the record," the judge said. "Dr. Brown, you have testified for the prosecution in so many cases, it is impossible that you did not know your remark was improper. I hereby hold you in contempt and will determine the punishment after this trial is concluded. Do you understand?"

The jury's stares were fixed on O'Bannon, as if he were a criminal. Which, in my opinion, he was.

"Yes, Your Honor," Dr. Brown replied to the judge, his eyes down. His expert witness racket had just come to an abrupt stop. Similar to, but even more costly than the end of my leash.

I continued. I would now clean what was left of Dr. Brown's filleted corpse.

"If I understand your statement, you determined Betty was lying because she quickly answered questions about her age, name and that she was the defendant in this case. That's all you had as a basis of a damning opinion, correct?"

"Perhaps I was a bit hasty, perhaps mistaken," he said.

"Your oath to tell the truth, perhaps that oath was a mistake?" Even I didn't understand exactly what I meant by it, it just rolled out.

"Well," he said miserably.

I wanted to make sure the jury would recall where this disgraced expert came from.

"How many times have you appeared as an expert witness for Mr. O'Bannon over the past three years?"

"A few," he said.

"Just a few?" I raised my voice in apparent disbelief. Brown's face contorted, knowing what was coming.

"Doctor that is another deliberate lie. You are on record as having testified as an expert for the prosecution in more than twenty-six cases in the past three years alone. If you dispute this number, I will be glad to provide the proof. Do you dispute this number?"

"No," he said, in a hoarse whisper.

"Have you testified as an expert on behalf of the defense in any criminal case?" I asked. "Have you ever testified on behalf of *any* accused person, such as Betty?"

"No," he said.

"What is your total income for testifying for Mr. O'Bannon?"

"Approximately $60,000 for my testimony in twenty-six trials during the past three years," he answered, wrongly assuming I knew it and could challenge him if he didn't use the correct figure. The beauty of destroying a witness is the fear they develop. That fear keeps them on track. "I charge $1,000 for an initial interview with each defendant," he said.

"You were paid $1,000 for ten minutes with Betty, a rate of $6,000 per hour. And how many times in Mr. O'Bannon's twenty-six cases did you testify the defendant was lying?"

"I'm not sure," he answered.

I picked up a piece of paper and pretended to start around the podium to show him something. He assumed the worst and held up his hand defensively.

"I suppose I testified each one of them was lying," he said.

"You concluded Betty was lying because she was too composed and responded too readily to your questions. And you assumed that because Mr. O'Bannon had told you that?" I asked and held my breath.

And he gave it to me. "Yes," he said.

"Dr. Brown, I have the transcripts from the last twenty-six cases, and in each case, your testimony is exactly the same as your testimony against Betty. You stated in each case the defendant was lying based on the fact that he or she was far too composed and responded too easily to your questions without hesitation. Do you recall using the same exact words in every case for the last three years at least?"

"No," he answered. Then thought better. "But perhaps I

did so subconsciously."

Again, I walked directly up in front of him, as close as possible without violating Judge Blevin's unwritten rules about not crowding a witness.

"I am handing you a copy of a portion of the transcript of your testimony in one of those cases. I now ask that you read it to determine whether it refreshes your memory." I handed it to him.

Dr. Brown took a few minutes to read the transcript and visibly shrank as he laid the papers on his lap.

"Please tell the jury what you testified under oath about the defendant being a liar?" I requested.

His answer came hard for him. "I said the defendant was far too composed and responded too easily to my questions without the hesitation normal for someone so accused."

Brown was openly drenched in sweat, his face beet red. I was concerned that he was about to suffer a heart attack. But I felt only anger that he had done his best to convict Betty, just as he had all the others.

"Dr. Brown, you have told this jury this basis for finding Betty lied was perhaps unconsciously also used in twenty-six prior cases. Then you admitted it was this prosecutor who told you that Betty had been far too composed and responded too easily to his questions without normal hesitation. His and your use of this exact same phrase is deliberate, not subconscious, isn't that true?

His answer "yes" was now loud enough for everyone to hear.

You took $60,000 in blood money to send those twenty six defendants to prison with that exact phrase, and the two of you are trying to send Betty to prison with the same lie, aren't you?

He was a broken man in the witness chair. His apprehensive response of "yes" was no less than a plea for mercy.

"Dr. Brown, let's address one more issue. Your report states that Betty's testimony that Waterman raped her with a shotgun was – and I quote – 'overblown and an attempt to justify her killing him.' The report goes on to say that the insertion of a shotgun barrel into the vagina once or twice – and here I quote again – would not represent a sufficiently injurious act to cause a woman to suffer an irresistible impulse. Do you recall writing that?"

To say the jury was now frowning openly would be an understatement. An attorney once told me, "If I had handed the jury a hatchet, they would have finished the job."

"Would you like to reconsider your opinions about the use of a shotgun to rape a woman?" I asked.

He shifted in his seat. "Perhaps with more understanding of the facts ..." he trailed off lamely.

"How about the callouses and scarring?" I asked.

"The what?"

"Did Mr. O'Bannon tell you the medical examination confirmed the rapes had been so numerous that there were callouses and scarring?" I let the jury see my grimace.

"I did not know that," he answered.

"Let me ask you a final question, Dr. Brown. In light of everything you've considered today in this courtroom, would you like to withdraw your expert report?" I held it up in my left hand.

He almost literally jumped at the chance. "That might be the best course of action."

"I need the record to be clear, sir." I paused, "Is your answer, 'Yes, I would like to withdraw my report'?"

"I would like to withdraw my report," he said.

I closed my notebook. "I will pass Dr. Brown, the witness of Prosecutor Jerry O'Bannon back to Mr. O'Bannon for redirect." I made sure those names were linked together in the jury's memory.

I looked at Betty. A single tear was sliding down her cheek as she looked back at me, grinning. I wanted to hug her in that moment in celebration, and she was letting me know she wanted the same thing. I exulted in the feeling.

CHAPTER 37

Ira Waterman for the Prosecution

In what could only be described as desperation, after the abysmal performance of Dr. Brown, Jerry O'Bannon called Ira Waterman to the stand.

The tide had not just shifted. It had run out, stranding O'Bannon on an island.

I was shaping a cross-exam in my head to go with my substantive notes. I assumed O'Bannon would show Waterman was a grieving father of the victim.

Ira Waterman exceeded my expectations. He swaggered to the witness stand, all three hundred pounds of pugnacity.

O'Bannon, somewhat stiff behind the podium, began his direct examination.

"There has been a great deal of testimony in this case alleging that your son abused the defendant and his daughter, Beth," O'Bannon said. "Tell the jury what you know about Sam's relationship with defendant."

The man turned ostentatiously to the jury, and held up his index finger like a lecturer's pointer. "He loved Betty and did nothin' to her that was not appropriate. She refused to perform her wifely duties!" he snapped.

He was off and running. "My Sam loved Betty since high school and was tremendously proud when she married him. The baby was on the way right after they tied the knot and he was excited. He's a good son, and his mother and I have always been proud of him. He was a great athlete in high school and has worked in my construction company since graduation, making a very good living and providing very well for his family."

O'Bannon tried to lead him into safety. "But their marriage was troubled?"

"Yeah," Waterman went on, "within just a couple of weeks of getting married, Sam said Betty had turned cold toward him and refused him. He wanted to know what he could do. I told him to wait for the baby to come, and then he'd need to persuade her, if you get my drift, to do what a wife should.

"But that woman always was strange. Sam was her man. She knew the law – the man's the ruler in the house and bedroom. I think she just done it to aggravate him."

"Did you observe a change after the child was born?" O'Bannon asked.

"I didn't since Sam hardly ever brought her over. Sam, he told me he'd straightened her out and she'd quit denying him."

"Did the defendant ever complain to you about any abuse?" O'Bannon asked.

"Not one time," he answered and stabbed the air with

his finger. "Never. Seemed all was settled, once she got used to it."

O'Bannon continued. "Well, did you see or hear anything that could be called abnormal or unusual, in terms of violence in the marriage?"

If the question had been a basketball, it would have clunked off the rim. Multiple rapes with a shotgun was abnormal, but O'Bannon just didn't see that because he was stuck on the old 'marital exception doesn't apply in Michigan' issue. That's a congenital defect in some lawyers' makeup. They just don't know when they've lost an issue. They keep beating the dead horse.

"No," Ira said. "Far as I could tell, it was a normal marriage after he settled the rules."

O'Bannon turned to the next issue – Evelyn's damning testimony about the murder plot to kill Betty and Beth.

"Your wife, Evelyn, has testified that Sam planned to kill Betty and Beth and you were aware of that plan. Is that true?"

"Course not," Ira said. "Evelyn's got signs of dementia these days you know? You can't believe a word that woman says."

O'Bannon said, "Thank you, sir," as if Waterman were a 'sir' and as if Waterman had stated something believable. He passed the witness.

I felt solid as I rose and stood at the podium.

"Mr. Waterman, did you believe that your son made a mistake, marrying Betty?" I asked.

"No," Ira said.

"That's not what you told my investigator, is it? You told him that Sam was better than that bitch he married, didn't you say that?"

It was as though Ira grew larger in the chair. He stuck his jaw and his chest out.

"Well, yes, that is true, if I said it." His answer might have been a good response to my inquiry, if he'd just left it there. Of course, he didn't.

His voice raised. "She was so high and mighty, all that stuff refusing to be a wife to my son, he had to straighten her out."

"Did Sam say what he had done to straighten her out, as you say?" I kept it simple.

"Sam told me he had to apply some good old-fashioned persuasion."

"And what would that persuasion be?" I asked.

He hesitated. Then he said it, as if to prove himself right. "Well, there was the shotgun. That was what done the trick."

The shotgun had become a cornerstone of the case, and I knew I didn't need to dwell on it anymore. For the rest of their lives, the jury would think of the case every time anyone mentioned the word 'shotgun'.

"You actually told my investigator you expected Sam to kill her and that you were astonished to hear that she had shot Sam, isn't that the truth?" I stuck my chin out a bit, too.

"I never said that," he blustered.

"I am going to play what you said on this tape recorder and then ask you to explain your answer to the jury," I said.

The quality of the tape was good. The jury all leaned forward to listen, anyway. "When I heard she killed him, I couldn't believe it. I was sure he'd be the one doing the killing."

I started to ask another question, but he beat me to it.

He shouted at me, "Because you are all acting as though that bitch had a right to kill my son, and no one has stood up for him to this jury."

I took a breath to keep my cool.

"Mr. Waterman, do you recall telling my investigator that Sam was planning on killing Betty and that he had planned to do it in a way where she would just disappear with the child so he could get himself a proper woman?"

"Yes, but that don't mean he would have done it. What could he do, tied up in a marriage with a little brat crying all the time and a woman who refused to have wifely sex with him, except when he forced her? He told me what he had to do to make her perform and how tough she was, fighting him off until he jammed his gun into her while that little brat screamed and cried. He told me he was damned if he would give her a divorce because she'd blab to the whole town about him. I told him not to worry. He was just doing what any husband would do, and it wasn't against the law."

I asked, "From what you are telling this jury, you actually approved of his jamming his gun into her to force sex, is that correct?"

"I sure did. He had to cut her down to size from that high and mighty pose of hers. She thought she was better than the rest of us, her college education and her airs, and all. She was his wife, dammit. He only did what he had to do. She was playing the field herself and his buddy Joe Stone told him about it."

I asked the court to strike the last remark.

"It is hearsay," I said.

Judge Blevin sustained my objection.

"Did you tell my investigator that Sam called his daughter Beth a whining brat who cried and screamed when he was forcing her mother to have sex with him?" I asked.

Ira was fully committed at this point.

"Sure, I did, and it was true because he told me what a pain the little brat was with her crying and screaming every single time he pointed that barrel at her mother. I still can't believe she got the drop on him. The bitch got lucky."

"We have heard testimony that Sam met with you on October third, the day before he was killed, and told you about his plan to kill Betty and Beth the next day. Is that correct?" I asked.

"Is that from Evelyn? She lies all the time."

"Why would you think it was Evelyn?" I asked.

"Because she was there with Sam and me when we were

just speculating on what he might do to clear the way for a proper woman, so it must have been her," he said.

That was an unearned run, but I took it. He'd just placed Evelyn at the conversation, gave her testimony a foundation.

"Mr. Waterman, is it true you gave the keys to your backhoe to Sam and told him you would have your partner, Joe Stone, pour the cement floor of the barn over the graves where Sam intended to bury Betty and Beth?"

"We were only kiddin' around," Ira said. "I told him he could use the backhoe and equipment on site and agreed that Joe would do the cement work, but it was Elsa who egged him on. But it was only kidding."

"What did Elsa do to help this so-called, kidding-around plan?" I asked.

"She said she'd get the plastic for the trunk of her car," he said, "and the gas for burning Betty's car."

"Mr. Waterman," I said, "you really expect the jury to believe Sam was only kidding around with the backhoe, the plastic, the cement and gas to burn the car?"

He sat silently, deciding which way to go. Retreat or charge.

I went on. "There's really no question Sam thought Betty deserved to die, or that Sam intended to do what he called 'the Betty job' the next day?" I sneered a bit, taunting a bit, to see if I could draw him out.

"Okay, you're damn right she deserved it," he said, sticking out his chin more. "What of it? I just wanted him to be happy with the right woman, not that bitch over there."

"You just raised your hand and swore to tell the truth to this jury," I said. "You then testified under oath that he was happy with her and always talked in a loving way about her and Beth. You testified it was a normal, loving marriage, and you never saw or heard anything that could be called abnormal. Now you admit he called her a bitch, he told you he wanted to kill her and kidded about a plan in very specific terms. That is all correct, isn't it?"

"Yes," he said, this time grudgingly.

"You have been lying to us all along about Sam's marriage, haven't you?" I said.

"I have told the truth about her failure to provide her wifely duties and the fact that Sam had to work extra hard to force her to do what the law requires," he answered.

"You believe Sam's jamming his shotgun into her was what the law requires, don't you?" I waited.

"Hell, yes!" he finally shouted. "What else could he do? She fought him, and he had to let 'er know she couldn't act that way."

Jim had been one hundred percent accurate in his assessment that Waterman was actually proud of his son. I gave the jury a look, then O'Bannon.

"Mr. O'Bannon, I give this witness back to you. He is your witness." I put enough emphasis on the word "your" for two of the jurors to spontaneously shake their heads.

O'Bannon's body language was a picture of absolute dejection. Both of his star witnesses had been huge gifts to the defense.

He called his last rebuttal witness, Joe Stone, to the stand. After the obligatory preliminary questions, O'Bannon tried to get something helpful out of Stone. It backfired.

Stone must have heard something about Dr. Brown being held in contempt. Then he'd probably passed Ira Waterman coming into the courtroom. Stone was smart enough to read body language and know what he had to do.

O'Bannon asked Stone about his friendship with Sam Waterman. He replied, "I was a close friend of Sam Waterman and have been for a number of years. It is my understanding that I am here to testify regarding what I know about Betty Waterman's partying and sex with other men during her marriage with Sam."

O'Bannon asked what he knew and Joe started to answer, talking about his "understanding" of Betty's behavior.

I objected before he could say anything else.

"Hearsay objection, Your Honor," I said. "If this witness

plans to tell us he simply heard something someone said, that's hearsay."

Blevin sustained the objection. "Ladies and gentlemen, I am going to strike this witness's last statement. There is no foundation for what he said. You are to disregard that answer – as you did Dr. Brown's answer that was stricken."

Blevin looked pointedly at O'Bannon, as he added the bit about Dr. Brown. The judge's look was silent, but it was a warning. 'Every time you try that, I'm going to make you pay in front of the jury.'

O'Bannon finished weakly, and passed the witness.

I rose from my chair, smiled at Stone, who got the message something was about to happen to him and I was going to enjoy it.

CHAPTER 38

Defense Cross of Joe Stone

Stone eyed me warily.

I began my cross-exam, homing in on his partnership in Ira Waterman's construction company.

Stone had agreed to invest $30,000 in the company. He hadn't paid Waterman. He confirmed his investment was past due. He admitted Waterman was pressing him hard to pay up.

I knew Stone had heard about the prior witnesses, and he'd seen Blevin's warning look at O'Bannon. I could see it in his eye he knew he'd walked into something and was worried.

When a witness gets that worried look, you can play on it. I didn't know what he'd say, but I took a swing at a ball outside the strike zone and connected.

"Tell us about the deal you made with Mr. Waterman to testify," I said calmly, confidently, as if I knew.

"Well," he considered for a moment, and then tossed in the towel. "When I told Ira I couldn't come up with the thirty thousand right now, he made me an offer. He said he'd carry me for a while if I'd testify about Betty having sex and partying with men in motels."

"Do you personally know anything about any partying and sex by Betty outside the marriage?" I asked.

"No I do not," he answered.

"What do you know about Betty Morse?" I asked.

"I haven't seen her in years, but what I remember of Betty in high school is she was aces high in Darien," he said.

"Tell the jury what that means," I said. When you want to make sure the jury is listening, you use that phrase.

"It means she was a straight shooter, a smart and quiet person." He didn't tell that she had dated me. He'd kept it clean.

I asked if he remembered October 5, the day after Sam was killed. He nodded, and said, "I was scheduled to pour the cement floor on the barn that day but couldn't do the job because the dirt hadn't been tamped down yet."

"How often did Sam work the backhoe?" I asked.

"He didn't use the backhoe," he answered. "Ira just said Sam would that day, and told me to shut up when I asked about it. It was a hurry-up plan."

"Pass the witness," I said.

Judge Blevin called for the noon-hour break. As he left the bench, he appeared to stop and look in O'Bannon's direction. He shook his head.

The judge in any case is like the guy with the top hat and fancy clothes at the circus. It's rare for a juror to miss the slightest thing the judge does.

The shake of a judge's head is like a thunderclap.

CHAPTER 39

Prosecutor Attacks Bob Nichols

As he did each time he went on the record, Judge Blevin started by asking whether there was any issue needing the Court's attention before bringing the jury back to the courtroom.

O'Bannon asked for a meeting in chambers.

As I closed the door to Judge Blevin's private office, O'Bannon went on the attack.

"Your Honor, there has been a breach of ethics so significant that it undermines the integrity of this trial," he said.

I'd prepared for this. It was the investigation report I'd found in the attorney conference room months before.

He claimed I'd violated ethics rules, taken advantage of the prosecution, done everything but spit in church. He wanted me cited as in contempt of court and admonished before the jury for improper conduct.

"I may need to ask for a mistrial, your honor," he finished.

I waited him out on his harangue and then went on the offensive. I told the judge how I happened to have a copy of the report after it was apparently discarded in a public place.

"There is no court rule preventing Mr. O'Bannon sharing that report. In fact, most of the prosecutors in Michigan recognize the need to share information including exculpatory evidence for the defense to ensure justice is achieved in each case."

I added that the federal rules of prosecutorial disclosure actually required sharing to achieve justice.

Then I got personal.

"When I worked for Mr. O'Bannon as assistant prosecutor, I voluntarily shared information with defense counsel in every case I tried. I consider the prosecutor's refusal to share information to be in direct violation of his responsibility under due process.

"Furthermore, there was nothing in the report that was not already known by both sides in the case. When I picked it up, I took a quick look and saw no indication that it included strategy or witnesses. If it did, I would have ensured it got back to the opposition. If I had considered it unethical to take or use it in those circumstances, I would have disclosed that to the prosecutor and this Court. But it was obviously a simple recitation of Betty's story and nothing else."

Judge Blevin had apparently dealt with the problem of sharing before because he addressed O'Bannon with a simple question: "Mr. O'Bannon, please try to convince me that sharing this information would not improve the chances for justice in this case?

"I have indicated to you for some time that your refusal to make fair disclosures conflicts with constitutional due process. It is part of your job as an elected prosecutor. The only reason there is no court ruling so far is the fact that no defense attorney has challenged your refusal. If there is going to be someone who is disciplined for this event, it will be you. I suggest you stop complaining about defense counsel's appropriate action and get back to trying this case."

I thought O'Bannon was going to have a heart attack on the spot. He stormed out of the office before I could get up from my chair, and I followed him into the courtroom knowing that I had an implacable enemy who would be looking for ways to hurt me forever in the future.

I also knew I had a judge who believed in his oath to conduct a fair trial.

Blevin brought the jury back in, and gestured to O'Bannon. "Any other witnesses, Mr. O'Bannon?"

"The prosecution rests," O'Bannon said.

Blevin looked to me.

"The defense rests," I said.

Blevin turned to the jury and addressed them with a louder tone, to make sure they heard clearly.

"We have come to the final arguments for the prosecution and the defense," Judge Blevin said. "The prosecutor will go first followed by the defense and the prosecution's rebuttal. Mr. Prosecutor, are you ready to proceed with your final argument?"

"Yes, Your Honor."

CHAPTER 40

Prosecution's Final Argument

"Ladies and gentlemen of the jury," O'Bannon started, "I know that you are as appalled as I am at the testimony of Ira Waterman. I join with you in being disgusted at the level of spouse abuse the defense has placed before you. I feel great sympathy for the defendant having been subjected to it."

It was a rational start. But the rationality was short-lived. O'Bannon had been hurt by the rulings, by his own witnesses, and by my very obvious demeanor of satisfaction at that point. He could restrain himself no longer. He went after me.

"Despite the silver-tongued, desperate razzle-dazzle of Mr. Nichols, the existence of spouse abuse is not a basis for self-defense when the abused spouse had the clear opportunity to leave the home with the child.

"According to the law, the use of lethal force is only allowed to prevent imminent harm. But in this case, the victim was sound asleep and posed no immediate threat whatsoever. There was no need for Mrs. Waterman to kill her husband in order to save herself or her child. She had access to the keys to the car, and the Michigan State Police post was a short drive away. Mr. Nichols would have you believe there's no relevance in a wife refusing to perform her duties for her husband. He proposes that any abuse is too much regardless of Michigan law, which does not penalize marital abuse. He is an officer of this court, and his attack on the law is disreputable and dishonest. He knows his arguments are improper but persists in them regardless of the law."

He was rolling now, enveloped in a cloud of his own grandstanding fumes.

"It is inconceivable that Betty could not have found protection from the police. Mr. Nichols knows it but employs a senseless argument that she was unable to take advantage of that protection because she supposedly feared her husband would follow and harm her and the child.

"We are faced with choices all the time, and the defendant, a brilliant student and graduate of one of our most prestigious state universities, knew or should have known that help was available. She chose to kill instead, and the blood of her husband is on her hands.

"Your question must be: Why did she kill rather than run? Mr. Nichols can posture until the cows come home, but the answer is obvious and refutes self-defense. There is no valid reason she killed her husband in cold blood."

I thought three of the jurors grimaced as he said that. O'Bannon didn't notice and plowed on.

"Betty Waterman," he raised his voice and pointed his finger in an unintended mimicry of Ira Waterman's finger, "is guilty of murder in the first degree. Going into that bedroom and picking up the gun proves premeditation.

"For god's sake," he shook his finger, "the man was

asleep!

"The defense of irresistible impulse is one of those flim-flam distractions Mr. Nichols uses to give support to this woman's self-defense claim. He would have you believe she could not stop herself. But isn't it obvious she would never have been required to stop in the first place if she had just left the home with her child when she had the opportunity? Her husband was sound asleep, for god's sake. Dr. Brown, a psychiatrist with years of specialized experience, examined her and told you she was lying. How did he know? He relied upon his vast experience in the field and called it as he saw it."

At the mention of Brown, there was a look of near consternation from one juror, as if to say, 'Are you really quoting that liar?'

O'Bannon finished with a flourish. "You are asked to believe the incredible and ridiculous notion that the defendant had no intention of killing Sam Waterman when she walked into their bedroom. There is no truth in that.

"The people demand a verdict of guilty of first-degree murder because it has been proven beyond a reasonable doubt that this woman walked into that bedroom fully intending to end her husband's life. She did so without the slightest legal provocation."

He sat down with a flourish.

CHAPTER 41

The Defense Debate

Iwaited for the jury to get over O'Bannon's brazen last statement.

"Without the *slightest* provocation ... Really?" I echoed, before I even got to the podium. I wanted to play off the absurd notion that shotgun rapes were not the "slightest provocation."

O'Bannon had missed his chance to offer a plea deal on the lesser charge. He'd ignored our experts without comment. He'd called on Ira Waterman, who'd antagonized everyone. He'd tried to prove Betty was lying based on falsified testimony by Dr. Brown. He'd been off balance during much of the trial. He'd antagonized Judge Blevin, the unofficial foreman of the jury.

The net effect was that we had a real chance with the jury. We had been handed a gift by an unprepared prosecutor.

But the fumes, I reminded myself, don't sniff your own fumes, no matter how great you think the trial is smelling. My general approach toward trials was you should take the plea deal you want before trial, if it's offered. I don't know where I developed the rule, but it reflects the karmic nature of an uncertain world.

I had to make the decision now. The decision was made somewhat easier by the fact O'Bannon had never offered manslaughter and never mentioned it during trial. Still, the lesser charge was an argument I could raise in my closing argument. I could couch it in the squirrelly language some defense attorneys rely on: "Ladies and gentlemen, if you aren't sure what to do, you can always fall back on the lesser included defense."

I had an essential aversion to that argument, which basically gutted the notion of justice and replaced it with deal-making.

Life is a deal. You can buy low or buy high. At trial, the jury sets the price, and the problem is you don't know what price they've set. It's an educated guess, the trial lawyer's educated guess. But it's the client who pays the price.

That's where the guilt of law practice comes in. You're playing with someone else's life. If you have any conscience at all, it's a high ante.

I had spent the better part of a day with Rob, Jim and Betty, debating whether to ask the jury for a manslaughter verdict as a compromise between total acquittal and first-degree murder. Juries have a tendency to split the baby. In Betty's case, a manslaughter conviction would carry a maximum sentence of fifteen years.

My belief was that Judge Blevin would actually impose a substantially shorter sentence than fifteen years, if she were convicted on the lesser charge, because of the circumstances surrounding the case.

But I also had a secret belief that a complete acquittal was possible. That was the rub, and I described it to our group.

If I suggested manslaughter in my closing, any waffling juror would grasp the option and eliminate any chance of acquittal. It would be a tacit admission that Betty killed

Sam and deserved some penalty.

Rob and Jim thought the prosecution case, which focused on Betty's failure to flee when she had the chance, remained strong no matter how much sympathy we'd injected into the trial. They wanted me to include manslaughter in my closing argument.

I tended to disagree with them. Which means I was lost in the deep woods of the most important decision I'd ever make. If I guessed wrong, Betty's life and my life would be forever changed for the worst. Our mini-jury was hung. The decision came down to Betty's opinion.

I wanted a last chance to talk to her.

"Your Honor, may we have five minutes to consult before I deliver my closing argument?"

"Certainly," he agreed. He motioned to the bailiff. "Ladies and gentlemen, we are approaching the end of the trial. We will take a short recess. During the recess, you are not to discuss the case, because you have not heard all the arguments." He motioned the bailiff to lead them out.

Five minutes later, I was still lost in the woods. We returned to court, and I asked for a recess until the following morning. "Your Honor, it's after four, and I confess I'm sore and tired," I said, "and I anticipate my closing will take at least an hour."

Blevin granted my request. We went back into the conference room, but I asked Rob, Jim, and Betty for some time so I could think over our options.

Betty smiled at me with those gleaming, trusting eyes. "Bob, I think we know we should go for acquittal, don't we?"

I touched her cheek and said, "I'm lost in the woods, Betty. I need to clear my head."

She touched my hand with her own. "Of course, we'll see in the morning."

CHAPTER 42

Over the Woods and Into the River

I left the courthouse and drove home with my mind churning as I thought through the closing. I was still focused on trial strategy and the final lines of testimony O'Bannon had presented.

I was feeling a sense of hope, but every muscle in my body was tense. The stress gnawed in my gut. The gunshot scar in my chest pulled my skin.

It was a beautiful early June day, sunny, a slight breeze, seventy degrees. It was the sort of day that reminded me of skipping school. I walked down to the river. The water was up and the breeze carried the clean green smell of the trees on the bank.

I changed into swimming trunks and a sweatshirt. I slid my pride and joy, my Old Town canoe, into the water. It was a wood and canvas canoe in Old Town's classic design, and it floated like a bubble on the surface. I took the first stroke with my paddle, and moved effortlessly out into the current.

I could always find peace and time for reflection in my canoe. I loved the northern Michigan rivers and took pleasure that my canoe gave me access on a moment's notice.

The water was moving briskly, and I turned and headed upstream, out in the middle, away from the river's edge, into the cleanest part of the water. A shallow rapids splashed down the main stream, and I stroked through it.

A large sord of mallards paddled ahead of me, nervous but not flushing. Songbirds were a chorus, and an old mossy-backed snapper sunbathed on the end of a large sweeper log.

The sun was still warm, although the shadows of evening were starting to spread across the water. The sun was visible only where the river bank dipped. A slight breeze created a riffle on the river. I kept paddling upstream, then let the canoe bow swing around with the current until I was headed downstream.

As I steadied the course with my paddle, Betty came back into my mind.

That summer after graduation from high school, she and I had spent hours canoeing. We'd put in and head up or down stream, it didn't matter. We could paddle for miles without getting tired. The last time, we'd been so innocent and in love we didn't bother thinking. We simply glided into the riverbank that day, and glided off into separate lives.

Dusk was calming, the water was calming, and I was daydreaming, practically asleep, when my canoe turned sharply as it slipped into the flume around the sweeper jutting out of the bank. I switched my paddle to straighten up, but it was too late. The canoe turned end-for-end, stern first downriver for several seconds, then flipped, throwing me under the tangled branches and matted undergrowth beneath the next sweeper.

The tangle below the surface suddenly was a net above me. There was a jumble of plastic and debris trapped with me. There seemed no way to get out as I clawed to get above the junk to the surface. I grabbed everything, but nothing held. The plastic debris snagged around my arms and legs. Nothing was solid enough to hold.

As the last bit of air burned from my lungs, I snagged a branch strong enough to hold my weight and with my last effort pulled my head above water.

It had happened so suddenly – an idyll reduced to panic. I hung by the branch, resting, catching my breath, shaken, as the current swirled past. I'd inhaled the riverbank run-off and tasted chemicals. One arm was still trapped by a mesh of some sort of plastic. I wanted to scream at every idiot who ever dumped crap into my river.

The canoe was hung up beside me but I jimmied it free, pushed it past the sweeper and then caught it, pushing it into the bank. I struggled to find footing in the mud of the bank, but the environment seemed suddenly alien, no longer natural. When I finally managed to crawl on hands and knees into the slime of shore, I was covered with ugly-smelling farm waste and manure. Slipping and sliding, pulling the submerged Old Town behind me, I gained enough ground to flip it, emptying a good portion of the water.

I lay back, panting, cursing, thankful for having cheated death.

Back in the house, I stripped, showered, pulled on some sweats and walked fresh into the kitchen. I poured a glass of cabernet and took out some food. It all seemed strangely new.

On the deck in the fading light, I set the bottle, glass, and cheese board down. From the deck the river looked as always, a serene surface reflecting the beauty around it and carrying my thoughts with it. In that moment, Betty's memory hit my core with a force. I had loved her then, and more now, and the thought of losing her again was unbearable.

The power of the feeling was almost disorienting, and I closed my eyes. I reached my hand for the wine glass and drank, then willed my eyes to remain closed until I heard a cardinal. I exhaled and felt my lungs inside my chest relax. There was one thing I knew in that moment, and it was a good thing, and everything else left my mind.

"I love her," I said to the gathering dusk, speaking to myself. Her face illuminated my mind. Whatever she needed, I would do, and whatever happened, I was prepared to take care of her.

I was out of the woods. I knew that for sure. There is something about sureness. It's as if the world encircles you in its wide arms and you can close your eyes against its bosom. I leaned back, took another sip of wine. I wondered what she was thinking at that same moment. I thought I knew.

The trial lawyer's task never changes, but the vision of what the task means can change completely. I couldn't wait to do my closing statement to the jury, and I was completely devoted to acquittal.

Me, the evening, the river, the bottle. I went to bed relaxed to the point where sleep came fast.

The next morning, I put on my best dark blue suit and darker blue tie, set off against a starched light blue shirt. There I was in the mirror, tying the tie, smiling at how pleased my mother would be of my attire. She would even be more pleased that I'd committed myself, come hell or high water, to Betty.

Driving into the city, I repeated my new mantra from the river in time with a song's pounding drumbeat on the radio. Focus, focus, focus!

We met for less than five minutes and I told them I

was with Betty's decision to seek acquittal and ignore manslaughter.

We entered the courtroom a little before ten.

Betty and I had collaborated on her outfits for the trial, going for the understated look – a dress well below her knees, subdued earrings, no jewelry. Attractive, but not threatening.

The bailiff brought in the jury. As if the whole world was in sync, the jurors were all dressed perceptibly better than they'd been on the first day of trial.

There's a saying, a happy jury is a defendant's jury. I had a secret belief that a defendant's jury was one that was lifted somehow by the experience. This jury, perhaps subconsciously, was dressed as if going to church, as if proud of the jury experience.

I believe the best jury is a jury that shows it has belief. I scanned their faces, and saw them looking back, composed and ready. They knew what they were doing and I had an odd sense of security that we were doing the same thing.

CHAPTER 43

Defense's Closing Argument

Judge Blevin addressed the jury, "I hope you all had a good night's sleep and are ready to proceed." He always made some small effort to touch a jury, which not coincidentally would be part of his constituency in the next election.

He motioned for me to proceed, "Counsel."

The equanimity I'd reached the prior evening notwithstanding, there were butterflies in my belly. I walked to the front of the lectern and faced the jury without notes. I wanted eye contact.

I wanted to remind the jury where we'd left off the previous day, and I wanted to start with a jab at O'Bannon.

"Without the slightest provocation," I said, and focused my eyes one by one down the line of jurors.

"The prosecutor said some unkind things about me,

which are unimportant. This is the first time I have ever heard the truth called razzle-dazzle and flimflam." I shrugged my shoulders.

"But no matter," I said dismissively.

"I am in a strange position after hearing Mr. O'Bannon's deliberate mischaracterization of the evidence. Apparently, Mr. O'Bannon believes colorful language can be used to disguise a complete lack of evidence for the prosecution. In his closing, he attempted to obscure the most important question you have to determine. That question is, are the facts that we have presented to you true. As Judge Blevin will instruct you, you are the judges of the facts and it is you who will decide what is the truth.

"Think about the testimony you've heard presented by the prosecution. Do you remember the chief prosecution witness, Dr. Arti Brown, the $60,000 paid expert, who took the stand, raised his right hand and swore to tell the truth and nothing but the truth, so help him God, and then proceeded to violate that oath with a series of lies in an astonishing compendium of perjury?"

I wanted to kick myself. 'Compendium'? Why did that stilted word come out of my mouth? I thought, "Keep it simple stupid!"

"Do you remember that man's false testimony?" I paused, hoping to emphasize what I was asking them, that I was one of them.

"As the prosecution's liar-in-chief, he and he alone testified Betty was lying." I would not call Betty 'the defendant' ever again.

"You should disregard the unsupported arguments of Dr. Brown and the prosecutor.

"That charlatan, masquerading as a psychiatrist, started with a lie about how much time he spent with Betty. Do you remember? 'I spent at least two hours with her at the jail.' That's what he said and then admitted it was false. He finally admitted he had lied to you about the length of time, and that it was *Betty Waterman* telling the truth, not him.

"He lied to you when he described the extended examination of Betty he claimed to have conducted, and finally admitted he had lied again when he testified that he based his conclusion on the manner in which she answered his questions. 'Too calm,' he said. He confessed he took $60,000 in blood money from this prosecutor to send twenty-six defendants to prison with that exact phrase, and that the two of them are now trying to send Betty to prison with the same lie."

"Doesn't it make you wonder about those twenty-six poor souls and what happened to them? Doesn't it make you wonder? Did the lawyers of those poor souls manage to expose the lies of Dr. Arti Brown with the knowledge of the prosecuting attorney or did they get away with it?"

I let that stand in the silence for a second, then started to drill into the jurors' personal stake in the trial.

"Does that false testimony help explain how important your role as a jury is to this woman, to our community, and to the nation?"

It was a big concept, but this case was big enough to carry the weight of concepts.

"Mr. O'Bannon, you know, is the one who paid for Dr. Brown's testimony. Even after the defense showed proof of Dr. Brown's repeated perjury, Mr. O'Bannon hailed Dr. Brown's testimony in his closing statement. 'Dr. Brown,' he said, 'relied upon his vast experience in the field and called it as he saw it.' Think of that. The prosecutor actually endorsed a witness Judge Blevin held in contempt."

I cast a look in O'Bannon's direction. When you stab someone in trial, you might as well drive the blade home. O'Bannon didn't have the courage to look up.

I was on. "Ladies and gentlemen, we have been offered lie after lie by this prosecutor. We have listened to witness after witness say this prosecutor wanted them to testify a certain way. And then we have seen these witnesses admit something different.

"Dr. Brown withdrew his false report. Do you recall that?" I asked, and several of them nodded.

"You've seen the prosecution witness sweat and withdraw a report, and say they were pushed to testify to something that they didn't know."

I held my palms open as if to catch the jury's answer. They were all with me now, and nodding.

"Is that what a trial is about? Lies?" I asked.

"Does that sound like it fits with our search for justice? Should the prosecutor have that kind of power in our community?

"What is our core belief? Innocent until proven guilty." I shook my head in agreement with myself for emphasis. "Do we want to live in a society where justice is replaced by the power of the lie?" I was hitting the burden of proof issue, without saying so.

"Do you remember also that Dr. Brown only testifies for the prosecution for money? *Lots* of money. The $6,000-per-hour witness. Do we want to live in a country where the truth is for sale to the highest bidder?" I wrinkled my forehead in disapproval.

"Prosecutor O'Bannon presented a paid witness to you as an expert on truth, and that witness admitted he didn't know the truth. Judge Blevin charged you with the responsibility to listen only to the testimony given and not the statements of counsel when deciding your verdict."

I turned sideways and gestured directly at O'Bannon. "This prosecutor lied to you, and we have proven his lies. Betty told the truth.

"Now I need to talk about Ira Waterman, who lied repeatedly to you until forced to admit his perjury. He was actually proud of his son's abuse of Betty. Prosecutor O'Bannon called him as his witness knowing he was lying because he had already heard Evelyn's and Jim Drew's testimony. Ira was the second prosecution witness who lied repeatedly with the full support and knowledge of this prosecutor.

"Then Joe Stone." I adjusted the lectern, just for some

change in the jury's attention. I was pressing the time limit for a good closing.

"Joe Stone told the truth about Ira's attempt to force him to lie about Betty. So, the question is this: If the prosecution calls a witness who admits he intended to lie because he owed $30,000 – do you think the prosecutor knew what was going on with that witness?"

Now I stopped, breathed and waited. They were still with me. I had the right rhythm.

"I think you know. I think you know the prosecutor in this case can't win with the truth. He can only win by lying." I lightly thumped the lectern.

"Tell me this: Where is the prosecution's truthful evidence that Betty is actually guilty? Truthful evidence," I repeated for emphasis. "Not lies, but *truthful* evidence?"

Here was my hook for the jurors to hang their vote on. Something solid in the way of argument to acquit.

Betty's decision had been to go for acquittal. No argument for a lesser charge of manslaughter. She'd been calm when she said she wanted the truth and wanted me and didn't want to "wander off like last time," as she put it. She was thinking about our parting and lost years.

I felt a surge of conviction from her decision.

"Tell me," I said to the jury, "where is the evidence that Betty meant to kill Sam Waterman? Where is the evidence she even pulled the trigger? It is nowhere to be found, is it?

"What we know is that Betty was overwhelmed, standing there with her toddler strong in her thoughts – the tiny little girl Sam Waterman was going to put in the incinerator – and the shotgun in the other. She heard a loud sound in her head and then blacked out. The next thing she saw was Sam, who was a bloody mess on the bed."

I paused, then said, "Where is the evidence she pulled the trigger? Did something else happen? Did Sam wake up and grab the gun and cause it to go off?

"Judge Blevin is going to instruct you," I said. "He is going to explain the prosecutor's burden of proof."

I held up my notes, as if they contained something important.

"Prosecutor O'Bannon called his witnesses knowing they were perjuring themselves and then lied to support them. He didn't carry the burden of proof. He instead carried the burden of lies. Did you notice that he has never mentioned Sam and Ira's murder plan for Betty and Beth?

"There is a sound of words, and there is a sound of missing words." I hoped that made sense.

"The prosecution of this case was simply based on a smear campaign – false accusations that Betty lied, false allegations that she partied at a motel, false allegations that she deserved to be raped."

I picked up the shotgun that was lying on the evidence table. It was wrapped in plastic. Holding it carefully with both hands, I pointed it over the jury's head so they would not be threatened, yet close enough that the barrel would be the center of their view.

"The prosecutor never mentioned this shotgun or the biologics evidence on it, did he?" They were rapt. "He mentioned is as a weapon used against Sam Waterman. But what about the fact that it was used as a weapon for years on Betty?"

I tipped the shotgun as if examining some part of it. "Do you think using this shotgun – like Sam Waterman used it – was an injurious weapon?" I timed the question internally before going on.

"Do you think this weapon – as used by Sam Waterman – inflicted injury on Betty's mind?" I asked.

"And do you think those injuries left scars?"

And now for the answer I wanted them to imprint. "And do you think those scars in Betty's mind were what made that deafening scream that overwhelmed her as she stood thinking about imminent death for her daughter and herself?"

By the end of a trial, you have an animal sense of the air in the courtroom. There are full silences, there are bored silences, there are all kinds. Now, I heard the loud silence, the jury's engagement with the theory I was describing.

"We have approached the defense in this case using only the truth, but the prosecutor has failed to present any truthful evidence that Betty premeditated her husband's death.

"We do not believe that just because Sam Waterman was a rapist or a potential madman, he could be killed without punishment or consequence. Michigan law does not permit execution for heinous crimes. However, what we believe is this: Sam Waterman damaged Betty's mind so severely that her mind was incapable of competent thought. She could not flee, she could not maintain control, she could not think clearly because of the screaming inside her head that was caused by the emotional scars of Sam Waterman's horrible abuse.

"What did she do? We don't know. It could be she simply held the shotgun as Sam Waterman effectively pulled the trigger. It could be self-defense. It could be an irresistible impulse that caused the gun to discharge."

I set the shotgun carefully back on the evidence table. I wiped my hands on my pants as I turned to the jury.

"All we know is the prosecution chose not to present truthful evidence of what happened. Instead, the prosecution ignored Betty's uncontradicted testimony that she went into the bedroom in an attempt to convince Sam to let her and Beth go."

I was acutely aware of time now.

"This poor abused woman was prepared to promise she would never tell anyone about his abuse. She was not standing in that room premeditating murder. She was only premeditating how to talk him out of killing Beth.

"She did not grab the gun to shoot, but to keep him from shooting. As she stood beside the bed, in that moment, she realized that man would keep his promise, just like he always did with his buddies. He would kill her and her toddler that morning."

I started the next sentence, and paused for effect. "Now what is the most important thing …

"Did the prosecutor try to deny Betty was overwhelmed? Did he try to deny she heard that overwhelming sound in her head? Did he try to deny she closed her eyes?

"Did he say, 'she pulled that trigger intentionally?'" I rapped the lectern with my knuckles.

"Did he say any of that? Did any witness say it?"

At least four of them were shaking their heads, maybe five.

"You have heard the evidence proving that she told the truth about the rapes, the abuse, the shotgun, the threats to kill her and Beth. You heard the testimony about the plan to bury them at the construction site, the plastic wrap, the gasoline.

"You heard that, but what didn't you hear? You didn't hear a word about Betty pulling the trigger, now did you?"

I waited for their assent.

"That's because there is no evidence of that. Betty's mind was overwhelmed at that point. That's all we know. For Betty, if she pulled that trigger – and I am not at all saying she did, only 'if' she did – she was clearly under the irresistible circumstance that she described to you.

"When I asked her to tell you what was in her mind, she said: 'It was the overwhelming and terrible fear that he intended to kill my daughter, Beth, when he woke up that morning by throwing her into the furnace.' That is the same furnace where the remains of the kitten were found."

I walked back to where Betty was seated and put my hand on her shoulder, facing the jury.

"Judge Blevin will instruct you to use your common sense and experience. Think of Betty in her position at that moment," I continued. "Was she premeditating anything, or was she seeing her three-year-old daughter being thrust into the flames. With that vision in her head, was she in control when the gun discharged, killing Sam Waterman?"

I backed away from the lectern to finish. You only have

so much space to work with, but there is enough to reset the arch of the jury's attention and create focus.

"With regard to self-defense, we start with Betty's testimony that she believed without question that Sam intended to kill her daughter, Beth, that morning. We do not rely upon the simple fact that she had been systematically abused for three years. We rely upon the fact that Sam was fanatical about carrying out his promises. We rely on the certainty that she could not have escaped him without being hunted down and abused worse. We rely upon the absolute belief by Betty that he was going to kill her and her child that morning. We rely on Evelyn Waterman courageously stepping forward to testify about her son's evil plan to kill Betty and her granddaughter, Beth, that morning. We rely on Ira's testimony that Evelyn was there when the plan was discussed.

"If you want to know what actual truth is, consider this," I said. "Consider Evelyn Waterman's son is dead, yet her sense of justice remains. She stepped forward to tell the truth that he was planning to murder Betty."

I held up my notes. "There is truth in a trial, and you, the jury, are how we know the truth. As you deliberate, remember Evelyn Waterman and remember her truth. Her son is dead, but she is still committed to the truth.

"I know you will be determining the truth of Betty's and Evelyn's testimony in your deliberations, and I am confident you will find Betty has been telling the truth from the beginning of this case. Although the testimony she gave was about matters that happened in the privacy of their home, there is undisputed supporting evidence of her truthfulness found in the scars on her body and her mind.

"Sergeant Brasso told you they found the remains of Beth's kitten in the ashes of the furnace.

"Shawn Roberts, the biologics expert, testified he found fluid evidence that Sam Waterman did exactly what Betty described.

"The photographic evidence of Betty's face provides

more evidence that Sam Waterman did exactly what she said he did – beating her face the night before.

"Consider Ira Waterman's testimony that Sam admitted that he had jammed his gun into her to force sex. His testimony confirmed in every detail what Betty told you. He was the prosecution's witness. Even he had to admit the obvious facts.

"Did Betty have a reasonable belief that Sam was going to kill her and her toddler? His own father, Ira, testified that Sam had openly talked about killing them. Joe Stone confirmed some details, and Evelyn supplied more evidence of the plan. If that shotgun had not gone off that morning ...," I waited.

"If Sam Waterman had not died by a shotgun blast that morning, you know," and I looked at them hard, "you know where Betty and her daughter Beth would be now. Don't you?"

I paused, "We all know where they would be. They would be under that storage barn floor, down in the dirt for eternity, covered by a cement floor. We all know that, don't we?"

I put up my hand. "It is plain as day, isn't it? The only premeditated murder that we've heard about in this case is Sam Waterman's premeditation to murder his wife and a tiny girl." I would not say the daughter was his.

"That was a murder plan and the only murder plan in this case."

I said, "Thank you" without the other bits I typically used. I was done, the jury either had it or it didn't. I wound it up where I needed to.

I went back to my chair like a lawyer does at the end of closing argument, hopeful and empty. It can be a cruel job.

CHAPTER 44

Prosecutor's Final Rebuttal

The prosecution always has the last chance to address the jury with a rebuttal argument because the prosecution has the burden of proof. Truth be told, it's usually too late because the ship has already sailed.

A good rebuttal focuses on its best point and drives a nail through it.

O'Bannon had neither nails nor a hammer. His witnesses had been destroyed, and his bluster had suffered from Judge Blevin's legal rulings. O'Bannon was a one-trick pony.

He rose from his seat and walked to the rail of the jury box and stood, posture straight, nostrils flared, and a sweaty upper lip. His red face matched his bright red trial tie. He cleared his throat, then went where he always went. The personal attack.

He didn't disappoint. I'd started the trial out by angering O'Bannon, and I'd kept his anger fueled throughout.

"All the razzle-dazzle in the world," he started in a stage-announcement voice, unconsciously returning to rhetoric that had previously been cut off by Blevin. "All the razzle-dazzle," he repeated, "cannot change the fact that a man is dead and Betty Waterman killed him."

He paused theatrically. Only two jurors were even looking at him. The fact was lost on him.

"Mr. Nichols has tried to convince you that Sam was a terrible person. Even if true, it does not allow the defendant to murder him. She had the option of simply walking out of the house with her daughter and driving away, never to come back. No private citizen has the right to kill another just because that individual does not measure up to some standard. The state of Michigan has eliminated capital punishment even for violent criminals who have murdered over and over again. If the state of Michigan no longer has a death penalty, how can you righteously forgive the defendant in this case? She picked up a shotgun and killed a man in cold blood."

By the end of a trial – any trial – certain words and ideas have lost their usual meaning. They seem to have quotation marks around them. The word "shotgun" meant something to our jury, and I was pretty sure it meant "sexual assault on Betty." He was off to a bad start.

"Don't allow any sympathy you may feel for the defendant to confuse your thinking," he said. I looked at the jury's faces, and they were feeling anything but sympathy as the word "shotgun" lingered in their brains.

"I am confident," O'Bannon said, "that you will see through attorney Nichols's outrageous use of smoke and mirrors and find his client guilty of murder in the first degree because that is what the proofs have demonstrated, beyond any reasonable doubt. It is your sworn duty to disregard sympathy and find the defendant guilty as charged of first-degree murder."

He was finished and so was the trial. I sat at counsel table, completely drained. A trial is not a job. A trial is a created life. A story that is lived intensely over a compressed period of time. When a trial ends, it's as if a friend has passed, and there is an emptiness.

It was not over, of course. The biggest part was about to start – the jury deliberation. But my part was over. There was nothing more I could do. It was out of my hands. And "it" was the rest of my life. What the jury did with Betty, it would do to me.

After the most intense year of my life – this case, my practice, my feelings for Betty – there was nothing left but blind hope. I felt Betty's hand on my arm and realized I had slumped in my chair. Her touch brought me back to the courtroom. She smiled at me. I sat up and took her hand, feeling her warmth, as Judge Blevin cleared his throat to read the instructions to the jury.

CHAPTER 45

Judge Blevin's Charge to the Jury

The judge's charge to the jury was lengthy and encompassed both the basics and the nuances of the law.

Instructions are a set of terms and definitions that tell the jury *how* to think, but not *what* to think.

He told them they could not let sympathy influence their decision. He said they were the sole deciders of the facts and must determine which witnesses to believe or disbelieve. He said they should base their decisions on the evidence presented in the courtroom, not speculation. And that the defendant was presumed innocent; the prosecutor must prove each element of the crime beyond a reasonable doubt.

I thought I heard a barely perceptible, but notable emphasis on the term "beyond" and the term "reasonable doubt," but I was almost too tired to game out the weights and values.

He outlined the requirements for self-defense and irresistible impulse as defenses to the charge of murder. Then he said the jury could consider whether the defendant was guilty of the less serious crime of manslaughter.

The manslaughter mention seemed a non sequitur, because neither lawyer had mentioned it. For a moment, I thought several of the jurors' eyebrows went up in question. They briefly looked at me, and I pursed my lips, obviously rejecting the notion. I believed they saw it and understood the lesser charge was not my idea.

In that moment, I had a flare of adrenalin and fear followed by a flood of relief. I thought suddenly of the risk of not inviting the lesser charge, but that thought was immediately followed by the certainty that Betty had made the right choice. I would never be able to say how or why I knew, but I knew. I felt the pressure on my hand as Betty squeezed it. She had seen the body language exchange, and she knew, as well, what it meant.

Judge Blevin went on. "The verdict must be unanimous." He summarized, "You may return one of three verdicts: guilty of murder in the first degree, guilty of the less serious crime of manslaughter, or not guilty."

He concluded, "Ladies and gentlemen, the bailiff will now be sworn in, and then he will escort you back to the jury room."

They stood and walked quietly into the jury room as the bailiff held the door open, then closed it behind them.

CHAPTER 46

Waiting for the Verdict

I looked over at Rob and Ben, who had been allowed back in the courtroom after they testified. I asked them to join Betty, Jim, and me in the attorneys' room to talk.

They all took a seat and looked at me expectantly. I felt emotional. Each one had become a friend and given their all – Jim, of course, nearly giving his life. I told each one directly how much Betty owed them for their passionate defense and dedication. They acknowledged her gratitude but were quiet, the strain of waiting already taking hold.

We did what lawyers and clients always do while waiting for a verdict. We speculated, and we talked in hushed tones about alternate outcomes.

I told them I thought the jury was with us. Rob and Jim were more ambivalent. Betty was so drained she had no opinion, only hope.

I explained the range of possibilities. A verdict of manslaughter would allow Judge Blevin to sentence her at any level he wanted. I was sure the sentence would be miniscule compared with the required sentence of life for first-degree murder.

The charge of manslaughter did not fit the technical facts of Betty's actions, but juries have a habit of finding lesser charges when they sympathize with the defendant but are unwilling to acquit. The bloody photos of Sam might override all the legal niceties and jousting at trial. A man was dead, and Betty had held the gun that killed him.

I asked Jim, Rob and Ben to give Betty and me a little time together. They filed out, each formally shaking my hand with a strong grip, each grimly silent.

I took Betty in my arms and we held each other tightly. I whispered in her ear that I loved her. Our bodies were tight.

"I want to face the future together, no matter what the jury decides today," I said.

She pushed me gently away.

"No, Bob. There's only one way we'll face the future together. We have to be together. If I'm gone, I have to let you go, and you have to make a life without me."

"Betty, you have no choice," I said, and embraced her again. "If you love me, forget about fairness and just tell me. Will you marry me?"

She kissed me strongly and pressed her face to my shoulder. "Yes, oh yes, I love you with all my heart and I will marry you."

It was a moment I will never forget. My life was in my arms and the feeling was right. I started to describe our future – we'd marry as soon as the trial was over, no matter what happened, then I'd adopt Beth, and if the worst came to pass, I'd raise her until Betty got out.

"What are our chances ... of winning?" she finally asked.

"Better than we could have ever hoped at the beginning of this," I said. "We don't need to win anything. We just need not to lose. We need one juror to hang the jury. But in reality, we need enough numbers to get a clean acquittal.

"There's a middle ground where they could compromise on manslaughter if not enough want a clean acquittal.

All it takes is two or three of the strong ones to refuse to vote for acquittal, and that'll force the others to go to manslaughter.

"What's hopeful is I think they all listened." At the same time I said it, a nagging doubt entered my mind. "I think they locked onto every word for the entire trial. I think we convinced all of them that you were telling the complete truth. The worst manslaughter sentence is fifteen years, but the judge can give much less." I didn't mention a first-degree murder conviction.

"But, even if it's fifteen years," I said, looking her in the eye, "I will be there waiting for you, every single moment, every single day. We are young. Even after fifteen years, we will still have many, many years together. I love you with every fiber of my being."

"I know it will work out," she said. "You've been magnificent, but I am ready for whatever comes as long as Beth is in good hands. I'm at peace."

The words were good, but her whole body was trembling.

"I'll take care of both of you," I said. "I promise."

At that precise moment there was a loud bang on the jury room door, and my heart dropped so visibly and dramatically, Betty felt my body jerk.

"What's wrong?" she asked, as if something was wrong with me physically.

I had failed her. I knew it instantaneously. For the jury to have reached a verdict in thirty minutes, it could only be a guilty verdict. There simply wasn't enough time to sift the evidence and reach a unanimous decision. Darien was a conservative town with deep moral foundations. The idea of a gun murder being accepted was not a possibility.

I should have known better than to believe.

Remorse crashed in my head. It was self-recrimination for leading her, my client, to make the decision to ignore the manslaughter argument that had been possible.

The truth is that a lawyer never really lets the client make the decision. The words may come from the client's mouth, but something the lawyer says without words makes the decision, and the client just makes the sound of confirming words.

I had led Betty to a wrong decision. She had risked conviction on a first-degree murder charge because of what I'd conveyed to her. What was about to happen was my fault.

"Betty, a verdict this quick means only one thing. They found you guilty." I released her, stepped back. I hung my head.

Every bad thought I'd ever had about the law washed over me.

"Michigan law is horrible. The marital rape law is horrible. People in small towns can be cruel. I must have missed something." I could have gone on.

She stopped me. She moved back into my body and took my arms with her hands and made them embrace her.

"Remember me, your wife?" she said. "The woman who loves you and trusts you?"

I almost let the tears come out. "I'm just so sorry, so ..." I didn't know how to describe the feeling of an entire lifetime disappearing.

As we walked back into the courtroom, O'Bannon smirked so broadly, I thought he might break into outright laughter at the look on my face.

"Counsel," he said, as if greeting me respectfully. "How's it going?"

He was practically doing a little happy dance in his chair. I was standing beside the woman I loved, and she was facing fifteen years to life in prison.

O'Bannon knew what I knew. I had failed to make the required connection with the jury despite the evidence of terrible pain and suffering and psychotic abuse. Sam's murder plan had not been enough to sway the jury. I knew a better trial attorney would have won with what I had to work with.

I didn't respond to O'Bannon. I was too heartsick.

Judge Blevin took his seat. He didn't look at us. He knew

the same thing I knew. He looked different, troubled. What had happened wasn't his fault, and I would tell him that later.

He rapped his gavel for order before turning to the bailiff.

"We are back on the record. There's been a knock from the jury. All parties are present and I would like to ask the bailiff for the jury's communication."

CHAPTER 47

The Verdict

The jury walked in and took their seats. They looked at Betty and me. Instantly, I knew we had a chance. This jury was happy. They looked happy.

I felt relief, thinking that we had beaten the life sentence required for first-degree murder. I had a premonition the sentence would be months rather than years.

Judge Blevin said, "Will the foreman please identify himself?"

One of my two stood. I'd had him early on.

He cleared his throat. "I am."

The judge paused a moment to consider his words.

"Ladies and gentlemen, you have been attentive, and we have all appreciated the way you have conducted yourselves during this trial.

"Before you disclose your verdict today, I would like to make some comments," Blevin said. "The law limits our roles. Mine is limited to judging the law, the attorneys' roles are limited to presenting the evidence, and your role is limited to deciding the issues on the verdict form.

"Your verdict is not just a verdict. It serves as the conscience of the community. It goes far beyond a simple 'guilty' or 'not guilty.' It means something fundamental about society and people's conduct and the notions of due process. It says something about the rule of law. Let me pause just for a minute."

Blevin sat up straighter and adjusted the microphone. He was organizing his thoughts.

"When I was first out of law school, I clerked with a federal judge. Occasionally he would preside over naturalization proceedings. That's when citizens of other countries are sworn in and become citizens of the United States."

He glanced at the jury to see if they were following. Then he went on.

"Before he would swear them in, he would give the same little speech. Over the years, as I have aged, and as I have presided in this court, that speech has taken on more meaning."

He cleared his throat. "The judge would say, and I'll never forget this, 'the rule of law means our government is a government based on belief only, not on military strength.' He would say 'when our government changes, it changes because citizens honor the election, not because someone pointed a gun at someone's head.'"

He took a quick drink of water.

"You have a duty that you have apparently done well and done quickly. Once you deliver your verdict, your job under our system of law is done. Do you all understand what I am saying?"

In unison, they shook their heads.

"Counsel and I have conferred, and for the record we are all in agreement that the Court will receive your verdict as written. We will now proceed with the verdict." He stopped.

"Will the bailiff hand me the verdict?" He read it, handed it back, and the bailiff returned the verdict form to the foreman.

"Please go ahead and read the verdict, Mr. Foreman," Blevin said

He was still nervous, and cleared his throat. "Not guilty," he said, and mumbled under his breath, "for sure."

My relief was so strong, it felt like a blow to my solar plexus. I could hardly breathe. I momentarily found it difficult to stand. Betty turned to me with tears already forming and a look that almost buckled my knees.

O'Bannon rose and asked Blevin to poll the jury. It was a formal request to make sure it was unanimous. Judge Blevin asked each juror, in turn, to state whether they had reached the same verdict.

The first juror replied strongly, "Yes," she said, her voice bouncing off the courtroom walls.

Each one seemed to make an effort to be louder than the last. By juror number eleven, the sound had become almost a weapon, and the weapon was aimed directly at O'Bannon, who refused to look up.

Juror number twelve hesitated. There was a sudden silence. O'Bannon looked up to see what was going on, and juror number twelve – one of my two stalwarts from early on – looked him square in the face and spat out loudly, "Not guilty, sir!"

He raised his hands and jammed both thumbs downward. There was a collective laugh. An inside joke of the jury's that the rest of us would never know.

They all beamed at Betty.

My world collapsed into a sudden flush of victory and a flush of exhaustion.

Betty was crying. I turned to hug her.

As much as I had thought about innocence, I realized I had never let myself believe it was possible for the case to be over and Betty would be free to walk out with me.

O'Bannon and his assistants left as quickly as they could load their cardboard boxes, brushing by the reporter. He gave me a look of pure anger, and I knew the next time he would be intent on revenge. But this wasn't next time.

The jury spilled out of the box in a rush and gathered around us. Each of the women jurors came to Betty and hugged her unabashedly with a display of affection unlike anything I had ever seen in any courtroom and have never seen since.

They were in tears, telling Betty how deeply sorry for her they were and how proud they were of the verdict.

Each of the men came up to me with a strong hand-shake and said a simple, "Good job, Bob!"

A woman juror came to me and hugged me.

"Thank you for representing Betty," she said. "All of us felt that we were also on trial under that terrible law. We had to do something!"

Another joined us, and said, "You're going to make a great couple."

I thanked her and told the jury I had proposed and Betty accepted before the verdict was announced.

Our friends and the jurors erupted with congratulations. The jurors milled around the courtroom for at least half an hour, wanting to share their deep feelings.

Stella had been waiting in the attorney's room with Beth for the verdict, steeling herself for the possibility that it might be the last time for the toddler to see her mother for a very long time. They walked into the courtroom together, and Beth ran to her mother with a joyful scream.

It seemed Rob, Jim and Ben were all pounding me on the back at the same time they were hugging Betty. Everyone was thanking everyone else.

As we all left the courthouse, Evelyn stood in the exit by herself. She was smiling, her hands clasped in front of her dress.

Betty was the first to speak. "Evelyn, I will never forget your courage in testifying. I am sorry for the loss of your son, but I ..." and she paused, not knowing how to express the rest.

Evelyn had tears in her eyes. "I wasn't so courageous for all those years, honey, or it never would have come to this. I'm sorry for you and all he did to you. He was not my son any longer," she said and shrugged apologetically. "I know that sounds bad, but you can't love someone who does what those men did."

Evelyn held Betty's hand, obviously wanting to say more. "I'm sorry, I know this sounds bad, but I'm glad he's gone. I got to say this. Betty, you get married and you and Beth get rid of that name, Waterman. When I'm divorced, I'll change my name back. When that old man is dead, the name Waterman will be over and gone forever from this town."

She bowed her head, as if ashamed of what she'd said.

Betty hugged her and they walked out the door together.

We were a loose gaggle of happy folks with the dramatic verdict still lifting us up. Betty was holding Beth in her arms, and the toddler was hanging on with all her might. They were a picture that still flashes up in my mind now and then. A crowd of reporters standing at the entry level of the courthouse doors were clamoring for Betty to talk with them.

Suddenly someone in the crowd screamed, "He's got a gun! He's got a gun!"

The crowd parted like the Red Sea for Moses and there was Ira, standing at the foot of the stairs with a gun in his hand.

"You murdering slut!" he screamed. "You killed my son and you and your lying attorney got you off. Now I'm going to kill you and your brat."

Betty stopped as she faced him, carrying Beth tightly in front of her. It was obvious that any shot at her would hit Beth as well. I lunged forward in a futile effort to shield her, but he swept up his gun and shot Betty and Beth with one terrible shot before I could get in front of her. The gunshot was an explosion louder than anything I had ever heard, and my heart felt as though I had taken the bullet. I was almost looking down the barrel as he fired and had no hope for Betty and Beth. She and Beth were defenseless within eight feet before him with no chance that he could miss. I was too late to protect them from certain death.

Except that Evelyn was beside her, and in an act of incredible courage, she stepped in front of them and took the bullet. The impact of the shot propelled her against me, and we went down together.

She fell into my arms as I went to my knees in front of Betty, and I embraced her there. I saw Ira falling forward on the steps with blood pouring from his neck and chest. His gun fell from his hand, and I could see he was dead or dying. Evelyn was momentarily awake and asked me if Betty and Beth were all right. I made sure they were and then told her they were safe. She asked what happened to Ira. When I said he was dead, her only comment was, "Thank God, that's the end of those crazy, abusing Watermans. They are together in hell."

She leaned back against me with a long sigh and I thought she was gone. I tightened my grip, cradling her in my arms. She had saved the woman I loved from certain death, and I was in a state of rapture, unwilling to let go as though I could save her by hanging on. Betty was on her knees beside me, using her dress to press against the wound.

A huge crowd gathered around us as Ben pulled Evelyn away from me. I let go, but unwillingly, as he tore her dress away from the wound and attempted to staunch the blood. There was so much it scared me, and the crowd's gasp was loud and frightening. All of us were horrified by the extent of the wound and the immediate certainty she had given her life for Betty and Beth. My eyes started to burn. The misery of what one person could endure and still rise up caught in my mind and froze me in the midst of all that was happening.

I realized there had been two gunshots from behind me almost simultaneously with Ira's shot and found out that Jim had drawn and fired his gun in response. It didn't cross my mind until later that I would have been the next target if he had time to fire again.

It was only a few minutes before the EMT personnel stationed at the courthouse took over and put her in an ambulance. As it took off, we all piled into our cars and followed it to the hospital where we waited together for word on her chances. It was a grim and suspenseful wait. She had taken the bullet in the right of her chest as she moved in front of Betty. We had all seen the large amount of blood. It was an ugly wound, and as the time passed, we were growing more and more concerned.

Her action in saving Betty was so heroic it was awe-inspiring. We talked around and about it for most of an hour before the doctor reported the miraculous news she was going to survive. In an incredible stroke of luck, he said the bullet had not struck a vital organ. Her closest relative at that point was Betty, and the surgeon took her aside and gave her the particulars, which she then shared with the rest of us.

Evelyn had lost a lot of blood and her survival had seemed unlikely until the path of the bullet had been determined. We were virtually overcome with intense relief. Betty furnished her phone number and mine to the ICU nurses' station and indicated she was available at any time and we would be there in the morning. We headed home with the verdict substantially dampened by Evelyn's trauma and the gun battle with Ira on the courthouse steps. It had been such a brutal and sudden attack, there was no way to get it out of our minds. Evelyn's statement damning the Watermans was a particularly vivid window into her years of subjugation.

Jim was our hero again. He had saved my life when Elsa attacked in the courthouse and then saved Betty, Beth and me from what would have been certain death from Ira's next shots. He had drawn his gun in what seemed the blink of an eye and his two shots had been perfectly placed. Ira was dead before he could fire again. I had known Jim was permitted to carry a concealed gun as an ex-police officer, but he had never made anything of it in all our work together. It turned out he had been a top handgun marksman in the Michigan State Police before his accident. His shots had been immediate and lethal. Once again, he was there when needed most. I owed him more in friendship than I could ever repay.

Ira's death was a fitting end to the madness of the male Watermans — abusers at a level so extreme it had become psychotic. Ira's support and participation in Sam's plan to kill Betty and Beth had been so egregious his psychosis was obvious; his total lack of concern for human life was mind-blowing. The incredible courage of Evelyn, a thirty-year recipient of that abuse, was a response so far above expectations as to be unimaginable. Few people ever have the opportunity to display heroism, and even fewer take that chance when offered. Evelyn had shown what she was made of when she put her life on the line for her granddaughter and daughter-in-law.

I looked forward to her inclusion in the family and a chance to hug her long and hard for saving Betty and Beth and for her testimony which had introduced Sam's murder plan to the jury — a turning point in the trial at the very last moment. I could not imagine the words I would need to make her understand my debt of gratitude.

When I took Betty to my home that night, I was hoping she would like it. In fact, she loved it. Beth, too, admired her new bedroom and was asleep in a few minutes. Betty and I shared my bed that night, just holding each other and talking for a long time. I finally felt everything was right in the world. At least in my world. When I woke in the morning, Betty still in my arms, I felt the same way.

CHAPTER 48

Collateral

Damage

Of course, news of the trial – and O'Bannon's shameful ethics – was plastered on the front page for days. The news carried for weeks afterward as Judge Blevin brutally worked O'Bannon over regarding his trial conduct and apparent suborning of perjury. He managed to escape punishment but only by cooperating with the court to overturn all twenty-six of Dr. Brown's perjury-supported verdicts. Of course, O'Bannon blamed me, and it wasn't in his nature to forget and forgive.

Somehow, O'Bannon managed to win several more terms as prosecuting attorney but the word was out, and his lust for state party involvement had no takers. His hatred of me was well known and defendants wanted no part of that additional burden in their defense, particularly since the prosecutor is solely in control of plea deals.

It didn't matter. Mary began specializing in commercial law and I focused on representing plaintiffs in civil damage actions. My practice flourished after the news stories described my trial skills, perhaps unfairly flatteringly – I felt the credit really went to Jim Drew and Ron Willoby. But it was to my lasting advantage. New clients all seemed to have read all the news reports of the trial.

My attorney friends told me O'Bannon was stewing in his own juices, which was fine by me. As Rhett Butler told Scarlet with his semi-immortal words from *Gone with the Wind*, I flat out "didn't give a damn."

My finances suddenly became not only manageable but infused with new money. The practice was back in the black and Mary was a joy to work with. My great friend Stella was operating full blast as office manager, keeping us focused and joyfully running our lives. Neither of us complained.

After thirty years, Stella is still keeping the office operating and Mary has made a name for herself in commercial law. They made my retirement from the practice smooth, and I left them well situated, despite O'Bannon.

Dr. Brown found himself in more trouble than he had dished out for so long. Judge Blevin's contempt citation cost him a $5,000 fine and another front-page article. His license to practice was also pulled. I thought no punishment was good enough – if they had flogged him in the stocks and given me the whip, I would have perhaps been more satisfied. My anger at that sanctimonious son-of-a-bitch still burns after thirty years.

Elsa was convicted of attempted murder and sentenced to fifteen years in prison. But her mental instability almost immediately led to suicide, and I breathed a sigh of relief that any future threat to my family was gone.

Rob worked intensively with both Betty and Beth. Recovery was hard work, especially for young Beth, who suffered harrowing memories and recurring nightmares of her sadistic father. She slowly emerged from her shell and flowered into a chatty preschooler, student, then a young woman, with the same brilliance and warmth of her mother.

Jim Drew not only remained a friend, but he and his wife grew into part of our family. In fact, his son, Jim Drew

Jr., a year older than Beth, became her soul mate. He followed his dad into the Michigan State Police while Beth
became an attorney. In her third year of law school, she
had a baby – little Angie, the light of our lives.

Evelyn was Angie's doting grandma. As it turns out, she
was able to fully recover from the gunshot wound. Ira had
been at the foot of the stairs, and Evelyn had stood well
above him. His bullet penetrated at an upward angle above
her lung and heart below her shoulder. No bones had been
shattered and the surgery removing the bullet was successful. Evelyn lived every day as if it were her first.

Betty returned to the woman she was before marrying
that man. She dedicated her life to supporting and leading
a number of organizations, working to help women suffering from spousal abuse. Rob Willoby and his wife joined
forces with her to help raise funds for a safe house for battered women.

Ben Deering supervised Betty's reconstructive treatment, securing the services of a talented surgeon at the
University of Michigan. He stuck with us through the
whole process, helping us deal with all that went with the
abuse and injuries so we could become man and wife in all
senses. But from that start, there was always a fire between
us. Which brought my memory back to that kiss. That kiss
as we waited for the verdict.

CHAPTER 49

At Home

I could still feel the passion of that moment – the wave of love as I buried my eyes in Betty's auburn hair. That hair, the scent of her, the warmth of her pressed into me.

And then, crash! A whirlwind five-year-old granddaughter landed on my lap. I opened my eyes to Angie, who was staring up at me and grabbing my hand with a sticky fist. It must have been obvious I had been sleeping because I heard Beth, her mother, laugh.

"Wake up, Dad! Angie won't let you sleep anymore," she said.

"When did you get here, Beth?" I asked.

"About two minutes ago when Angie was heading for you at full speed. Where's mom?"

"She went grocery shopping for supper. I have been sitting here daydreaming, waiting for you and Jim to arrive."

As if on cue, Betty walked in with two big bags of groceries. I loosened Angie's tight grip around my thumb, set her down and moved to the kitchen. Betty had bought a huge prime rib, which she claimed there was time enough to finish before supper.

I slipped my arms around her and she hugged me in return. "I've been dreaming of the trial and how we kissed while waiting for the jury's verdict," I told her.

She laughed and gave me another kiss that carried the same, mesmerizing result. Standing in the kitchen of our home with the woman I loved after so many years, I realized for the thousandth time the agony of waiting for the jury's verdict when we had stood together, holding each other as though to keep the world away.

I nuzzled Betty's hair, tightening my embrace. She pulled her head away to look at me.

"What's with you?" she asked, a smile forming in the corner of her mouth.

"I love you." It was all I said, and I will admit my lip trembled. "Silly, aren't I?"

She knew exactly what I meant.

The End

EPILOGUE

This book is based on an actual trial which featured the mid-1950s acceptance and support of spouse abuse, derived from old English law and biblical reference. Rape of a wife was decriminalized in Michigan by what was called the marital exception rule (also referred to as marital exemption) – an abomination Michigan finally ended in 1989. Some shameful states still make a distinction between the rape of a spouse and the rape of anyone not a spouse. The Battered Women's (spouse) Syndrome is now recognized as a basis for evidence of such abuse but not as a reason for a lethal attack on the abusing spouse. Imminent threat or danger is still required for justifying self-defense.

Fortunately, support groups for abused women have sprung up everywhere. Reporting abuse has been assisted by police training and legislation requiring investigations based on observation of abuse, even when the battered woman is afraid or refuses to complain. In the old days, a woman was asked why she didn't simply leave her abusive husband. We have learned that it's unsafe, a step toward even more abuse or even death.

For almost fifty years after my case in Flint, self-defense was the legal defense of choice in cases where the batterer was killed in nonconfrontational circumstances, and the results were seldom effective for the battered wife. Reduction from first-degree murder to manslaughter was considered the "best" expected result, and judges meted out relatively long prison terms when there was a plea or conviction of manslaughter.

In the trial in Flint, Michigan, my use of two distinct and

separate defenses – self-defense and irresistible impulse (temporary insanity) – was a first-time, groundbreaking joinder of two essentially disparate defenses. The joinder allowed presentation of our evidence of massive spouse abuse against the prosecutor's strenuous motion to exclude it as a nonlegal support of self-defense where no immediate confrontation was involved. Although self-defense required imminent threat or danger, the irresistible impulse defense did not. So, the marriage of the two allowed me to get all of my evidence included.

I have not attempted to be factually accurate as to individual acts of abuse in that case, although rape and threats of death were involved. The kitten in her case was held in the door of the furnace while her child screamed and screamed. The shotgun was kept under the bed and used to threaten her. The husband was clearly psychotic and a truly frightening character.

In its final deliberations, the jury found it difficult to accept irresistible impulse as a complete defense because a recent murder trial in the county had been won by a plea of temporary insanity. The murder in question had been particularly gruesome, and the local press had described the not guilty verdict as a gross abuse of justice. Our jury compromised; it refused the prosecution's attempt to obtain a verdict of first-degree murder and found her guilty of the lesser crime of manslaughter. Our proofs of extraordinary spouse abuse led the judge to propose a sentence of probation without prison time. In an action stranger than fiction, my psychiatrist and I told the judge she was inconsolable about her guilt for killing him and needed some kind of punishment so she could atone. The judge agreed and gave her six months in the Detroit House of Correction, where she learned basic secretarial skills and came out to almost immediately finding a good job.

I wrote accurately of my own self-doubts as to my abilities when the jury signaled a verdict so quickly. I was nearly certain that I had failed to make the required connection to win. I admit my self-confidence was immeasurably strengthened by the jury's verdict. Our result was considered a stunning victory, particularly in light of the marital exception law. With the prosecutor and press having publicly stated their full confidence in getting a first-degree murder conviction, I enjoyed the fact that crow was a prominent item on their dinner plates. The anger of the prosecutor and his personal and continuing vendetta against me for his public humiliation and the public praise I received are accurately portrayed in the book. He never admitted that his reliance on a slam-dunk verdict had allowed my client to avoid life imprisonment.

I also did not have the love affair with my client. However, the trial got so much publicity, I was able to talk my flight instructor into breaking her hard-and-fast rule about not dating her students. She agreed to have coffee with me to discuss the ongoing trial. We were engaged soon afterward and married within just over a year from the verdict. So, the trial did support a love affair and a fifty-six-year marriage.

I am pleased the years have been even better for the Flint River. Dumping of waste has been almost completely eliminated. The high water of normal spring floods has scrubbed the formerly filthy banks clean. Deer feed on the lush vegetation beside the water, sheltered by the dense growth of plants and trees on the high banks. Sport fish and wildlife of all descriptions have returned to the much cooler and clearer water. The carp, still including occasional giants, obviously love it since they roll and splash in the shallow rapids. The river's smell is sweet and clean. Ducks and geese abound, and their persistent calling is a delightful addition to the river's chorus of songbirds.

ABOUT THE AUTHOR

Robert Steadman grew up near Syracuse, New York, the second oldest of five children. The family moved to Michigan, where his dad was hired as the state's financial controller. Bob graduated from Wayne University Law School in February of 1951, having earned his Bachelor of Arts, Bachelor of Law, and Juris Doctor degrees in five and a half years, all while working nights on the Ford River Rouge Plant's engine line. Drafted in May of 1951 for the Korean conflict, he completed Officer Candidate School and was discharged as a second lieutenant late in 1953.

Steadman had the good fortune of working one year with the best attorney in Flint and also a year as assistant prosecutor, an intensive introduction to trial work.

While learning to fly at Flint's Bishop Airport, he met and married his instructor, Bernice Trimble, already a famous racing pilot, in 1959. His aviation expertise led to a position as corporate and trial attorney for Airway Insurance Company in Ann Arbor, where he defended aviation death cases from Massachusetts to Alaska for several years. He turned down the company presidency in 1972 and chose to move to Traverse City instead.

Bob was eighty-one in 2009 when he tried and won his last jury case with an award of $400,000 for fraud against a local bank. He then cared for Bernice during her remaining years of illness until he lost her in 2015 after fifty-six wonderful years. Since 2018, he has served as president of Senior Center Friends in Traverse City, an advocacy group for the Traverse City Senior Center. He continues to enjoy pheasant hunting with his German shorthair pointer, Belle.

Made in the USA
Las Vegas, NV
16 February 2022

43978897R00144